2ⁿᵈ Edition

The Money Field

Three-In-One

Nelson Letshwene

The Money Field book series – 3-in-1

The Money Field

In the Game of Money, Everyone Is A Player, But Some Are More Skilled Than Others

R. Nelson Letshwene

Copyright© R. Nelson Letshwene, 2015, 2017

All rights reserved. This book is intellectual property protected by international copyright law. No part of this publication may be reproduced in any form without the prior written permission of the author and publisher, except in brief quotations embodied in critical articles and reviews.

Published by Moedi Publishing, a division of Moedi Learning Technologies.

Gaborone, Botswana.
Pretoria, South Africa

©R. Nelson Letshwene
PO BOX 80927, Gaborone, Botswana
nelslets@gmail.com / nelson@moedi.net
www.nelsonletshwene.com

CreateSpace Independent Publishing Platform
ISBN-13: 978-1978270060

ISBN-10: 1978270062

Moedi Publishing,
Moedi ISBN: 978-0-9870189-9-1
A division of Moedi Learning Technologies
Gaborone, Botswana
Pretoria, South Africa

DISCLAIMER:

This publication is designed to provide competent and reliable general information regarding the subject matter covered. However, it is published with the understanding that the author and publisher are not engaged in rendering legal, financial, or other professional advice. If legal, financial, or other expert assistance is required, the services of a professional should be sought. The author and publisher specifically disclaim any liability that is incurred from the use or application of the contents of this book.

DEDICATION

Yolisa and Ayanda Letshwene

You can't connect the dots looking forward; you can only connect them looking backwards. So, you have to trust that the dots will somehow connect in your future. You have to trust in something – your gut, destiny, life, karma, whatever. This approach has never let me down, and it has made all the difference in my life.

Steve Jobs

Table of Contents

DISCLAIMER: V

INTRODUCTION TO THE SERIES XIII

BOOK ONE – THE MONEY GAME 3

PREFACE 5

MAKING MONEY IS GOOD 5

1. INTRODUCTION TO PERSONAL FINANCE 9

2. DIMENSIONS OF PERSONAL FINANCE 13

3. AWARENESS, HONESTY, AND RESPONSIBILITY 23
    THE TRIANGULAR CODE 24
    AWARENESS 26
    HONESTY 29
    RESPONSIBILITY 32

4. YOUR MONEY FIELD 41

5. MONEY RULES ON THE FIELD 47
    1. The Income Rule *47*
    2. The Spending Rule *49*
    3. Borrowing for consumption rule *51*
    4 The Repayment Rule *53*
    5. The Budget rule or the "spending sheet" rule 56

6. MORE PLAYERS ON THE MONEY FIELD 59
    6. The Savings Rule *60*
    7. The Return of savings rule *64*
    8. The Money-In-Money-Out rule *65*
    9. The Borrow-For-Assets rule *67*
    10. The Repossession Rule *70*

    11. The Surrender Rule.. 71
7. THE VALUE OF AN INCOME 73
    1. The Value of an Income.. 74
    2. Who takes my money before I do?................. 76
    3. How often do you pay yourself?...................... 77

8. CONSUMER BEHAVIOUR 81
    The Commercialization of Our Senses 82
    Functional Literacy... 85

9. THE INTELLIGENT MONEY FIELD 91
    1. The Pay Yourself First Rule................................ 92
    2. The Return on Investments (ROI) Rule......... 95
    3. The Balanced Split Rule 96
    4. The Spider-Web Economic Doctrine............. 98

10. WHY IS IT DIFFICULT TO SAVE MONEY?... 101
    5. The Anti-Saving Obstacles 103
    6. Purposeful Saving..105

11. DEBT AND FINANCIAL INTELLIGENCE....... 109
    7. Do Financially Intelligent People Borrow Money?..110
    8. Borrowing for Security.......................................111
    9. Performing Assets Rule 115
    10. The Positive Cash Rule 116
    11. The Profit Rule or Income from Liabilities Rule 118
    12. The Sponsoring Rule 119
    13. Does My Income Exceed My Expenses?...122

12. POSITIVE CASH FLOW AND RE-INVESTMENT 125
    14. The Re-Investment Rule 126
    15. The Self-Sustenance Rule................................128

13. FINANCIAL GOALS 133

   SUCCESS THROUGH GOAL SETTING 133
   THE POWER OF WRITING DOWN YOUR GOALS 136
   SMART GOALS 138

BOOK 2 - LIVING IN THE GAP 144

INTRODUCTION TO BOOK 2 149

PREFACE 151

THE MONEY MANAGEMENT MODEL 151

1. LIVING IN THE GAP 155

2. BUDGETING PRINCIPLES 161
The Budget Spending Sheet 161
Your Annual Budget Principles: 164
Commitment 166
Principles 168
Prioritize and Categorise 169

3. PRINCIPLES OF SAVING 175
Pay yourself first 176
Your Money's Friends and Foes 178
Funding Your Emergencies 181

4. YOUR PERSONAL MONEY TREE 185
How Do You Find Your Own Money Tree? 187
Personal Skills Inventory 191

5. MARKETING YOUR PERSONAL SKILLS 195
Who Has Money to Give You? 196
Who Has Vested Interest? 199

6. HOME, SWEET HOME! 201
Start Early 203
The Buyer's Checklist 205

7. INFORMATION – THE PAPER TRAIL 209
Information Gathering: 211

Classification of Information *214*

8. PHYSICAL ARRANGEMENT OF INFORMATION 217
Choosing an Accounting Period...........................*221*
Information-Gathering Sheet................................*223*

9. CREATING RECORDS 225
Bank Reconciliation Statement.............................*226*
Cheque Book Balancing *227*
Section A: Income and Expense Statement.......*229*
Section B: Statement of Cash Flow......................*230*
Section C: Balance Sheet...*230*

BOOK 3 – THE TRAP OF OTHER PEOPLE'S MONEY 234

INTRODUCTION TO BOOK 3................................. 239

1. WHY DO PEOPLE WANT TO LEND YOU THEIR MONEY?... 243

2. OTHER PEOPLE'S MONEY 247
The Necessity of Debt?...*251*

3. TOOLS OF CREDIT 255
Secured vs. Unsecured Debt..................................*257*
Tools of Credit *258*
The Use and Misuse of Tools of Credit................*262*

4. THE FOUR ELEMENTS OF DEBT...................... 267
1. The Loan Amount 268
2. The Instalment Amount 270
3. Interest 271
4. Time 273

5. THE GAP PLANNING SYSTEM.......................... 277
The Flow of Your Money *278*
The Suggested Plan...*279*

6. DEBT STRATEGIES 283
Urgent Debt 284
The Cost of Debt 287
Debt Consolidation 289
What is Debt Restructuring? 292

7. DEBT MANAGEMENT PLAN 295
The Size of Debt Method 296
Commit to Your Why 301
Talk to Your Creditors 302
Letter to Creditors 304

8. THE STATE WE'RE IN 307

APPENDIX A 313

Q & A ON DEALING WITH PERSONAL DEBT ... 313
GENERAL DEBT QUESTIONS 313
CREDIT CARDS 319
CASH LOANS 324

ACKNOWLEDGEMENTS 329

ABOUT THE AUTHOR 331

BIBLIOGRAPHY 333

RECOMMENDED READING 337

OTHER BOOKS BY NELSON LETSHWENE .. 338

INTRODUCTION TO THE SERIES

The first edition of The Money Field was divided into three parts in the book. Because of the nature of the material in those parts, we have decided in this book to treat those parts as books, thus going from Book 1 (instead of Part 1), to Book 3.

The Kindle version of this book has actually been broken into a series of three separate books.

Book 1 in the series covers the basic principles of *The Money Field*, defining and illustrating it as a field upon which the game of money is played. It covers all the rules that are applicable in the game of money, along with the players that you get to meet on *The Money Field*. No one is ever alone on *The Money Field*. There are many players whose moves affect your own moves as in a game of chess. It is important to build your own winning strategy on your own Money

Field. The first book in the series will help you in understanding and applying the rules to your own game, and will conclude with money goals. Once goals are set, there is a gap between where you start and where you desire to end.

The second book in the series will cover practical strategies for living in the gap. Many people fail to meet their goals simply because they fail to live in the psychological gap between where they start and where they wish to end their goals. This gap requires practical strategies that will be covered in the second book in the series.

The third book of the series focuses on what we call "Other People's Money", or simply Debt Management Strategies. This will cover tools of debt or debt instruments used by lenders to get their money into your pocket. You in turn need to have effective strategies to get their money safely back to them without any damage having been done to you. It is more beneficial to you if you use other people's money to your advantage rather than to have them use you to grow their money. The third book will also cover the structure of debt and debt elimination strategies.

Added to the third book is an Appendix that

has Questions and Answers on debt instruments and debt strategies that one can apply in creating a Debt Management strategy.

Some of the material in this book was formerly published in the paperback book *Functional Mastery Over My Finances* (Reach publishers, 2008). Although some of the chapters that formed that book are in this book, they have been revamped, improved, updated, edited and made better for the sake of this new book series; and many other chapters of that book have been excluded.

The reason for this new book series was to clarify and add more to some of the concepts that were discussed in that book.

I have been blessed enough to "workshop" the material in this book series all over the country and the region.

Through these workshops I have met lots of people whose questions and concerns have helped to add more substance to this material and improve it.

In this book series I have also sought to encourage participation by including self-assessment questions at the end of each chapter.

I hope this book series will add value to the life of the reader, and help to increase financial literacy and other money skills that are so important in our lives.

If you enjoy this book series and find it helpful, and I hope that you will, I would appreciate a little feedback or brief review at your convenience.

Thank you,

Nelson Letshwene

Nelson Letshwene
October 2017
Gaborone, Botswana
nelson@moedi.net

The Money Game,

Everyone Is A Player, But Some Are More Skilled Than Others

Nelson Letshwene

The Money Field book series – 3-in-1

Book One – The Money Game

Nelson Letshwene

PREFACE

MAKING MONEY IS GOOD

"Opportunity is missed by most people because it is dressed in overalls and looks like work."
Thomas Edison

Money is a cornerstone of the human experience. We human beings have held and continue to hold dysfunctional beliefs about money. The time of change is now. Life was created for our enjoyment.
Money enables us to enjoy life. Money is not different from anything else in life – it is all energy, the energy of God, the omnipresent God, who fills all in all. There is no place God is not, including in money. To reject money is to reject something of life. To call money bad is to call energy bad.

Many people hold a dysfunctional view of money. Dysfunctional in that it is not helping them. It is not 'working' for them.

They hold the view that money is evil, and they are good, and therefore they repel money.

For how can that which is good attract that which is bad? They make money wrong, dirty, and unworthy. They call the rich, "stinking rich"; they call money "filthy lucre". They talk of "obscene profits".

It is this very idea that makes those who do "dirty jobs" make a lot of money, while those who do "good jobs" go begging.

The preachers and teachers of our children, and the scientists looking for a cure for AIDS go begging for money for their good deeds, while the dancers and players are splashed with money. Our psychology on money is backwards. It is time to have a right-side up attitude towards money.

It is fitting that every human being lives luxuriously. The earth has enough resources that we should all live luxuriously.

We as a species have however not yet learnt how to make that work. We have created an imbalanced world of the rich and the poor; few rich people and a majority living in abject poverty; and that, on a planet with resources that can feed all its inhabitants abundantly.

This book is to take you to places where your disempowering beliefs will be challenged, and opportunities will be handed back to you.

It seeks to help you to feel good about making money. It will help you to have a healthy respect for money; to stop shunning that which gives you life.

It is time to joyfully accept money for the services you render to humanity. Indeed, it is time to joyfully accept all good things in life, and joyfully share with others. Be not ashamed of money, for money perpetuates life. Welcome it into your life and allow it to stay with you.

Use money. Share money. Give money. Receive money. Give it love and it will love you. Do not criticize it. Praise it for what it is able to do for you. Invite it into your life. Live a life of appreciation for all good things. Making money is good. That which produces good is good. Love money for what money can do for you. Money gives you the ability to bring good to others. The good Samaritan wasn't broke! Mother Teresa, who did her good works among the poor wasn't broke! Yes, she was not greedy, but she was not broke! Her foundation is still bringing lots of good to the poor.

People may often say that money does not buy happiness; but haven't you noticed that when you have money you just seem to be a little happier than when you don't have it?

Welcome to *The Money Field*. Play to win.

Thank you

Chapter 1

1. INTRODUCTION TO PERSONAL FINANCE

"This is not a game where the guy with the 160 IQ beats the guy with the 130 IQ."
Warren Buffet

A life skill is practically a skill you should not go through life without. Personal Financial Management is a life skill! Why do so many people choose to go through life without mastering this skill?

You can "get away" with not having the skill to swim if your reason is that you stay too far from rivers and oceans, and that your country is land-locked. But how far can you run from money? Have you ever asked yourself?

- Where did all the money go?
- Have you ever wondered why budgets don't work?

- Have you ever wondered why you seem to have lost control over your finances?
- Have you ever wondered why, no matter what you do, you don't seem to be balancing your finances?
- Are you starting to believe that indeed 'the rich get richer and the poor get poorer', and that's just the way it is?
- Are you starting to believe that indeed money is the root of all evil?

Where do all such beliefs come from?

Indeed, many people are uncomfortable in the presence of cash, that's why they'd rather spend it. Many believe that money is evil, that's why they get rid of it, albeit subconsciously. Personal Financial management is an essential life skill:

- It is essential for you.
- It is essential for your children.
- It is essential for your friends and family.
- It is essential for anyone who has ever asked: where did all the money go?

The primary purpose of this book series is to give you the essential skill of managing your personal finances. Many people are intimidated by the financial lingo. They therefore stay away from financial books and financial conversations. Do not be afraid. We present this material in a language you can understand.

The fact is, everyone handles money, but not everyone is equipped with the skills necessary in handling money. Almost everyone uses credit, but not everyone is equipped to understand the language used by financial institutions and moneylenders.

Eliminate Your "I don't Knows"

The best way to understand this material or anything in life, is really to minimize your "I don't knows".

This allows you to begin making some decisions and see where they lead you. If you love your 'I-don't-knows', you will remain undecided, in which case you are likely to 'go with the flow'. But the truth is, you might not like where the flow is flowing to. An "I don't know", produces paralysis and fear.

So, the approach should be, "If I thought I knew the answer, what would it be?" While this approach does not say 'I know the answer', it gives you the opportunity to try different answers. It simply says, what if this was an answer, what effect would this have on the problem I am attempting to solve?

The problem of "right" and "wrong" answers exists only in schools. In real life, there are no "right" or "wrong" answers. There are events that produce outcomes. The reason schools have "right" and "wrong" answers is because they have to allocate marks and decide whether you have "passed" or "failed".

In the field of personal financial management, what is "right" for you may not necessarily be "right" for someone else. The answers are personal. Success is a personal thing.

Just as a disclaimer, we want to state here that no book can be a replacement for personal financial advice. Should you need personal advice, please utilize the services of a trained professional.

The field of personal finance is huge and no one book can cover all the material.

Welcome to this book series and I want to thank you for taking this precious opportunity to learn this ever-important subject of life.

Chapter 2

2. DIMENSIONS OF PERSONAL FINANCE

"An investment in knowledge pays the best interest."

Benjamin Franklin

> **LEARNING OUTCOMES:**
> In this chapter, you will learn to:
> - Identify the various dimensions of personal finance
> - Identify the seven essential money skills

Dimensions of personal finance represent various variables that influence people's relationship with money.

These variables are influenced by cultural, geo-political, economic, social, and personal preferences.

While there may be some general agreements among personal finance experts as to which behaviours would constitute what may be accepted as creating a more functional relationship with money, it remains the domain of each individual to determine what they do with their money.

The field of personal financial management covers a vast area of dimensions that are often neglected when dealing with the subject. The dimension of money, as depicted by the figure below, cover almost all areas of personal financial management:

DIMENSIONS OF MONEY

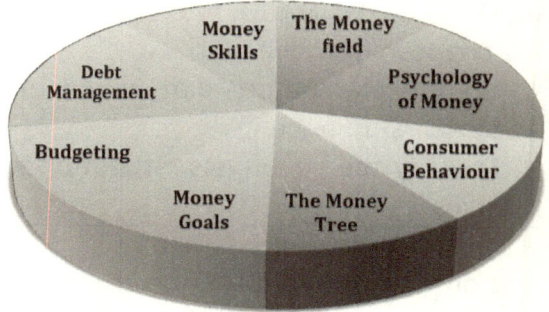

A brief description of each of the dimensions depicted in the dimensions of money diagram is included below. Going clockwise beginning with The Money Field:

1. *The Money Field*™ is what we define as a field of play upon which the game of money is played. This field consist of different players playing the money game, and you are one of them. In fact, everyone who handles money is a player on the money field. This is obviously the title of this book and will be covered in detail in the book.
2. *The Psychology of Money* covers our emotional involvement with money. Most people have a huge emotional body and it influences just about every decision they make. This also covers the beliefs we hold about money and how such beliefs affect our relationship with money. There is a whole book that I have devoted to this dimension called *The Psychology of Money – money follows the character of its owner*. (It should be published here soon – check amazon.com)
3. *Consumer Behaviour* is a subject that seeks to alert the consumer to their behaviours that leave them vulnerable to "sales tricks" or the attempts of marketers to get consumers to part with their hard-earned cash. As a consumer, it is vitally important to understand other

players on the money field and how they affect your money. I have often said, unfortunately the only people who do not understand consumer behaviour are the consumers. It is vitally important to know your money's friends and foes.

4. *The Money Tree*™ seeks to contradict the saying that "money does not grow on trees", and go on to show wealth-building systems used by the wealthy to build wealth. The saying that money doesn't grow on trees is a metaphor to emphasize that making money is hard. However, if you understand wealth building systems, and you go about setting them up, you are essentially, "planting money trees". If any person would dare to plant such money trees, they too could reap the fruit of their labour.

5. *Money Goals* is a dimension of personal finance that helps people to set financial goals and follow strategies to help them to reach their goals. The last chapter of Book 1 of this book series is devoted to this subject.

6. *Budgets* are normally the only dimension people focus on when they think they are working on their personal finances.

Unbeknown to many, they have left out a lot of dimensions that affect their finances. No wonder people conclude that budgets don't work. A budget is a tool that if used properly, could help the user to take charge of their finances. The chapter on Budgeting principles will give some guidelines on this subject.

7. *Debt Management* includes the entire realm of Debt planning, tools of credit, lending and borrowing guidelines, debt management, and debt elimination systems. Book 3 of this book series is dedicated to this important subject.

8. *Money Skills* is a huge dimension of personal finance as depicted by the diagram below:

MONEY SKILLS

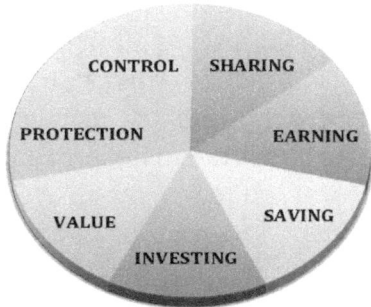

These Money Skills[1] are essential for anyone who wants to take charge of their finances. Each one of these skills are like a computer software that must be "installed" in the brain for it to start working or to become part of a person's psychic behaviour. A brief description of each of these is listed below. Going clockwise beginning with Earning:

1. *Earning* – this speaks of your ability to bring more money into your money field using your skills and talents. Most people generally use only one main skill to bring money into their money field. They leave a lot of skills and talents "unemployed".

   There are chapters in the second book of the series, which will focus on Your Personal Money Tree and Marketing your Personal Skills.

2. *Savings* – Everyone knows the importance of saving, but not everyone is able to practice this skill effectively. There are a number of pitfalls that stop people from saving. These are covered in the chapter called Why is it difficult to save money. Saving is a very important

---

[1] The details of these are the book *Seven Essential Money Skills* by R. Nelson Letshwene

first step in building wealth, and it is a very important skill to seek to master.

3. *Investment* – To invest is to put money away with an expectation of returns on your investments. Understanding the five investment systems and learning how to apply the learning practically is very important to mastering this skill. We will talk in this book about some of the processes necessary to implementing this skill on the money field.

In a separate book called *The Seven Essential Money Skills*, I cover all of these skills, and give more details to this particular skill.

4. *Value* – This skill speaks of your ability to create real value wherever you are. Understanding the time value of money and strategies that lead to growth is essential to mastering this skill. This is also an anti-waste skill. Learning to preserve your resources and not being wasteful leads to wealth accumulation and to growth. Many people are very wasteful, and therefore have to spend resources over and over again replacing today things that they bought yesterday. If they can only learn to preserve their

resources, they would not have to spend new resources to replace them. A book called *The Millionaire Next Door* by Drs Stanley and Danko sheds greater light on the behaviours of millionaires who build wealth.

5. *Protection* – Many people are very vulnerable to financial pressures. They are so exposed that it takes very little events to destabilize their entire financial life. Protection speaks of your ability to mitigate the risks you are exposed to through insurance and the creation of legal entities. There practically isn't a risk that cannot be insured against. Many people, however, do not understand insurance products and are therefore either under insured, or carrying wrong insurance products that don't apply to them. In a separate book called *Life Insurance and You – Demystifying* The Issues, I cover all issues relating to life insurance.

Legal entities are tools used by wealth builders to protect their wealth. It has been said that the rich own nothing, but control everything, and this, through the use of legal entities.

6. *Control* – This speaks of your ability to take charge of your financial life. Control is divided into physical control systems and building emotional controls.
Chapters in Book 2 covering The paper trail, Physical arrangement of data and Creating Records focus on the physical control element of this particular skill. The emotional controls, as has been mentioned, will be covered in greater details in the book *The Psychology of Money*.

7. *Sharing* – This is an integral part of human behaviour. Learning to share your money and resources without guilt and obligations is the key to mastering this skill. Many people share from a "wrong" attitude and therefore don't get the real benefits of sharing. Learning how the rich create "giving systems" or philanthropies is one of the ways of mastering this skill.

SELF-ASSESSMENT:

1. Name and briefly explain the various Dimensions of Personal Finance covered in this chapter.

2. Name and briefly explain the Seven Essential Money Skills covered in this chapter.

3. Which of the Seven Money Skills would you like to learn more about?[2]

---

[2] Learn more in the book *Seven Essential Money Skills* by R. Nelson Letshwene. Also available in the Kindle Store or in paperback on amazon.com

Chapter 3

3. AWARENESS, HONESTY, AND RESPONSIBILITY

"Until you are willing to take responsibility for all of it, you cannot change any of it"
Neale Donald Walsch

> **LEARNING OUTCOMES:**
> In this chapter you will learn:
> - The three core concepts of life
> - How to be more aware of your behaviour with money
> - How to be more honest with yourself about your true issues with money
> - How to take more responsibility in taking charge of your finances.

Before we go on to engage The Money Field in the next chapter, it is important that we examine the three core concepts that can prepare us. These are represented by The Triangular Code.

THE TRIANGULAR CODE

What is the Triangular Code?
The three core concepts of life: Awareness, Honesty, and Responsibility, have been called The Triangular Code[3].
We will go into details about these three, but let us first look at them from the psychological perspective.
In psychosocial systems the Triangular Code is represented by a triad:

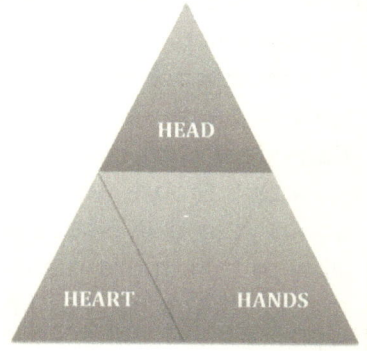

---

[3] Walsch, N.D, *Conversations with God*, Hodder & Stoughton

- AWARENESS, is a function of the HEAD.
- HONESTY, is a function of the HEART, and
- RESPONSIBILITY is represented by HANDS.
-

The HEAD represents awareness because it speaks of what you know about the subject at hand. It has been said that knowledge is power. I say what you don't know about money will hurt you.

When it comes to money, a lot of people don't *think* about money, but they *feel* about money! By skipping the head, your centre of awareness, and rushing to your heart, your emotions, you will be leaving an important part of your guiding system.

What makes us *act* before we *think*? It's the *emotions* from the heart! If you control your money with only your *emotions*, will you *act responsibly*?

If you *think* about your money more and increase your *awareness* about the subject, your emotions will be more controllable, which increases your level of *honesty*. The more honest you are about your money, the more responsible you become. Every responsible action you take also serves to increase your awareness, which continues to influence your emotions ... and the cycle goes on!

Money supports the character of its owner! We are here in large part not only to talk about money, but really to talk about its owner.

AWARENESS

What is awareness?

Awareness is what helps you to tap into your knowledge base. It is important before you comment on any subject to ask yourself honestly: what do you know about this subject?

Are you making an informed decision or an emotional decision? Is this an educated decision or an ignorant reaction? How wide is your field of vision here?

Many people are sleepwalkers. They are unaware at a conscious level of what is happening in many areas of their lives, not the least of which is Personal Finance. Awareness leads to wakefulness.

This book seeks to bring you to a full awareness of what role money is playing in your life, how you can take control and make sure that you play the game as you choose. Awareness is the first step to this process.

> Have you ever gone to an ATM, withdrew money, and two days later wonder what happened to the money?

Most of us have. The time between the withdrawing of the money and the asking of the question, 'where did my money go?', is what I refer to as *'the awareness gap'*.

You have lost awareness if you can't answer that question. It's like you withdrew the money, fell asleep, then woke up two days later with an empty purse. You just can't remember what you did with the money.

For some people, the awareness gap is as long as five years, or ten years, or even more. This is the time when you stop, look at your life and ask:

- What have I done with my money all these years?
- What have I been working for?
- What has my money done for me?

Perhaps now is that time. Most people don't ever ask themselves those questions because they are afraid of the answers that they might get.

So, they prefer to remain unaware. They

choose to stay asleep and never wake up. Now is the time to awake.

Give yourself all the facts, all the data about your life. Unless you give yourself all the facts, you are crippling your thinking process, and will therefore arrive at erroneous conclusions. For critical analysis to take place, you have to give yourself all the facts. You must be aware of what is going on. See things as they are, then you can make a decision to change them if they don't please you.

Bring yourself to full awareness:
- Are you aware of your habits and actions?
- Are you aware of your behaviours and emotions?
- Are you aware of your thoughts and your reasoning?

What habits and behaviours are propelling my money in the direction it is going? A habit is behaviour that you have done so many times that you don't have to think about it anymore. It has left the head, it is operated only from emotions and actions. There are various habits:
- Debt habits;
- Impulsive buying habits;
- Competitive habits;

- Saving habits;
- Investment habits; etc.

This question begins to tap on the root of the issue. Can you identify your habits?

HONESTY

Honesty speaks not only of truthfulness, but of integrity and openness. When I speak of truthfulness, I am not talking about you telling someone else the truth. In this instance, I am talking about you telling you the truth about you. If you can't disclose the whole truth to yourself, you have a bigger problem than you have imagined.

Integrity is the opinion you have of yourself. Not what you think others think about you, but what you are thinking about yourself. What is your opinion of yourself?

Here is an **Integrity test**: Answer yes or no.

PART 1:
1. Do you honour yourself?
2. Can you keep your own promises to yourself?
3. Can you say "no!" to harmful things to yourself?
4. Do you build yourself up?

5. Do you develop yourself?
6. Do you invest in yourself?
7. Are you growing?
8. Who are you?

PART 2

9. Do you sabotage yourself?
10. Do you always put yourself down and last?
11. Do you sacrifice yourself to try and please others?
12. *Do you spend money you do not have, to buy things you do not need, to impress people you don't even like?*
13. *Who are you?*

Count your "yes's" and your "no's". In the first part you should get as many "yes's" as possible, and in the second part you should get as many "no's" as possible.

For every "no" you got in the first part, figure out how you can correct that. For every "yes" you got in the second part, also, figure out how you can correct that.

Just remember that "the truth" does not exist as an objective reality. It is your truth you must always seek, not someone else's. Once you find your truth, don't try to compare it with the truths of others. Just live by your truth.

It is only when you are honest to yourself, and therefore become aware of your situation, that you can move on to the next step of taking responsibility. This is face-to-face with yourself! Can you face yourself? Literally! Can you stare at yourself in the mirror, eyeball to eyeball without getting uncomfortable with what you see? What are you going to do about what you are seeing?
You are hereby invited to meet yourself. Then you shall know yourself anew, like you have never known yourself before!
When you can feel compassion for yourself, then grace shall abound to fill your heart!

Honesty gives birth to openness. Openness of mind is the doorway to understanding and clarity. An open mind leads to light-heartedness that perceives no attack and therefore sees no need to be defensive.

"Nothing real can be threatened" ACIM[4]

Your real self knows this, and therefore is afraid of nothing.

---

[4] ACIM = A Course in Miracles. www.acim.org

RESPONSIBILITY

Responsibility speaks not only of duty, but of accountability and conscientiousness. The duty in responsibility comes in recognising your role in the outcomes or the aftermath of your life. Accountability speaks of your recognition of how your actions affect others, while conscientiousness speaks of your awareness in the entire process.

Responsibility means accepting the "blame" of it all. Not at all meaning that you should feel guilty – but knowing that you did it. Even if it was not all physically done by you, but that you had a role in it.

When you look at your situation, you will accept that you did it to yourself.

Sure, others may have contributed, but at the end, you did it to yourself. Perhaps it was in ignorance or unconsciousness, but still, when you awake, you realise that you did it to yourself.

This is where you come to the realisation that, as Walt Kelly's comic strip character Pogo said:

"We have met the enemy, and he is us."

Another author put it this way:

"Until you are willing to take responsibility for all of it, you can't begin to change any of it[5]"

Take a look at your finances. Who did it to you?

- Okay, the banks may have contributed;
- The moneylenders may have chipped in;
- Your relatives may have added something;
- Your employer may bear some responsibility;
- Your children perhaps?
- The government?
- The system?

But really, who did it to you?

Responsibility says, I have arranged the situations around me to produce the results that I now have.

---

[5] Walsch, N.D. *Conversations with God*

As long as you keep blaming others, you take your own power away from you. You are saying there is nothing you can do because you are not the one producing the results that you are observing. That is really disempowering yourself.

Taking responsibility might include something as simple as deciding to remove yourself from the situation that depresses you.

When we talk about taking personal responsibility in the area of personal finance, it will surely include some actions on your part. It may include taking the responsibility to work harder and find other ways of increasing your income. It will call you to make some tough decisions. But you must remember that only you can do that.

You can't keep walking around with a "woe is me" attitude if you are ever going to change. You will have to get out of your self-pity party, clean up the mess of the party, and start afresh. A declaration such as "I can do it" sets a tone for a new beginning.

You say, here is my financial situation, and I now take charge! All I need is guidance. Show me the map, let me identify where I am, let me decide where I want to go, and

let me take the first step!
- How can I make more money?
- How can I protect more of my money?
- How can I ensure that more of my money goes where I want it to go, that is how can I exercise more control?

Taking responsibility includes gathering information about yourself. You may start by asking:

"What is the source of my income?"

List all your regular sources of income and their frequency: Employment; Business; Dividends; Sales; Gifts; Other.

And, if you depend on borrowed money as income, also, list them. This allows you to see how much of other people's money you depend on: Loans; Overdraft facilities; Credit cards; etc.

> Many people are on a revolving credit system. You earn 10'000,00. You have a revolving credit from a credit card or overdraft facility of 5'000,00.
>
> You therefore *think* you live a lifestyle of 15'000,00. You are actually still living on 10'000,00 or less. Only in the first month when you used the "available credit" did your lifestyle go to 15'000. After that, you returned to 10'000. And now you are perpetually in debt to the tune of 5'000.
>
> At the end of every month, your account is at negative 5'000,00. Your salary of 10'000,00 comes in, fills up the hole and you have a positive balance of 5'000.00, and you spend the positive balance of 5'000,00; plus, the 5'000,00-revolving credit.
>
> The difference is of course that the additional 5'000,00 is borrowed money for consumption and it always comes at a cost. That cost reduces your lifestyle.
>
> If your salary should stop right now, you will remain in debt to the tune of 5'000 plus costs!

SELF-ASSESSMENT
1. What does Awareness mean to you?
2. What does Honesty mean to you?
3. Did you take the Integrity test? What elements of the test do you need to work on?
4. Are you a blame-shifter?
5. What will you do to take more responsibility in your finances?

Nelson Letshwene

Let the Games Begin!

Nelson Letshwene

Chapter 4

4. YOUR MONEY FIELD

"Money is only a tool. It will take you wherever you wish, but it will not replace you as the driver."
Ayn Rand

> LEARNING OUTCOMES
> In this chapter we introduce the following concepts:
> - The Money Field as a field of play
> - Different money rules as applied on the money field

There are different ways that people try to hold the idea of money in their lives. I use what I have come to call, "The money field™".

This field is made of the ingredients that almost everyone applies in their money game. I also see this as a game with rules. Our role is to understand the rules so that we can play the game and win. Look at this field and understand that you are already playing your money game on it, whether you know it or not. Understanding the flow of money on this field is the goal of this book.

There are four basic quadrants on the field of money as depicted in the diagram below. Every single person on earth operates on this field of money: the rich, the poor and everyone in between alike.

THE MONEY FIELD

INCOME	EXPENSES
ASSETS	LIABILITIES

This is the field of money upon which everyone who's ever handled money plays according to certain rules that are not written down, but somehow, they get adopted and applied.

Our rules of money are affected by many different factors including our upbringing, social standing, geopolitical factors, economic factors, and the society in which we live. Most importantly, however, our money behaviour is influenced by the beliefs that we hold to be true for ourselves.

Below are some of the rules that we will apply on the money field:
1. The Income or Earnings rule
2. The Spending rule
3. Borrowing for consumption
4. The Repayment rule
5. The Budget rule
6. The Savings rule
7. The Return on savings rule
8. The Borrowing for assets rule
9. The Repossession rule
10. The Surrender rule

For the most part, we all start at the same point. We start with nothing, facing the empty field. We start playing the game as soon as we have an income.

Take an example from the game of soccer. The size of the soccer field is standardized by FIFA (Fédération Internationale de Football Association). All the rules are also set by FIFA. Any team anywhere in the world, whether professional or amateur, will play on the same standardized pitch, applying the same rules.

There are no different set of rules for professional soccer players. There is no different size pitch for amateurs.

When the referee blows the whistle for the games to begin, the most skilful players know exactly what they need to do from that moment to the end of the game.

But if you put an amateur team or children on the soccer pitch that do not know the rules, it is entertaining to see how they all just follow the ball wherever it goes without any apparent coordination. If one of them scores they all celebrate, even if it's an own goal.

The Money Field is also a static, but invisible field upon which the game of money is played. The four quadrants of the money field are governed by standard rules for all the players.

The differentiating factor on the money field is the skill of the players. As the subtitle of this book says, in the game of money everyone is a player, but some are more skilled than others.

Because the money field is largely invisible, most people have no clue at any given time which quadrant they are in, and what the applicable rules for that quadrant are.

In this book, we have created this visual, so that you can always know where you are and what you are doing. We are players on this field in the game of money. This game has no reserves or benchwarmers. Everyone is in the field, playing their own game.

Some of us, when it comes to our money game, we are just like children on the soccer pitch. We do not know the rules so we just follow the money wherever it goes. Even when we score "own goals" we celebrate like children, until we are told that we have lost the game.

We celebrate when we get a personal loan and weep when we have to repay. We are reluctant to score real goals in building assets and love our quick fixes of quick loans.

Let us now spend some time learning some of the rules that are applicable on the money field. Let us observe our behaviour on the field and see whether we are winning the game. We will take each rule as it applies and see how we apply it in our games.

Let us begin.

SELF-ASSESSMENT

1. Describe The Money Field in your own words.
2. What affects the rules by which we play on the field?
3. Which are some of the rules that you look forward to learning more about?
4. What is the difference between professionals and amateur players on the field?

Chapter 5

5. MONEY RULES ON THE FIELD

"Money is a placebo, not a cure."
Richard Templar

LEARNING OUTCOMES
In this chapter you will learn:
- The Income Rule
- The Spending Rule
- Borrowing for consumption
- The Repayment Rule
- The Budget Rule
- How people get stuck in the debt cycle
---

1. The Income Rule

The first rule of money is the income rule. We all start at the point when money enters our field in the income quadrant. For most of us, that moment is when you receive your first income. At that moment, it's like the referee has just blown the whistle for the games to begin. It is reflected as arrow number 1 in the money field below (Figure A). Now the games can begin.

Figure A

INCOME → 1	EXPENSES
ASSETS	LIABILITIES

The Income Rule is important because without it, the game cannot begin in earnest. This income may be your salary or wages, it may be a gift or allowance.

What do you do when you receive your first income? Most people just do what is the most normal thing for them. Normalcy is a factor of our perception. We often do what we have seen other 'normal' people around us do.

We have earned our money and we feel proud. Now it's time for the next rule in our money game.

2. The Spending Rule

For many of us, the first thing we do, the next rule of money we apply is that when money comes in, money must go out.

This is the second arrow marked (2) in the money field below (Figure B). It is reflected in the expenses quadrant of the money field. You have now moved money from the income quadrant, to the expense quadrant, and it is never coming back!

Figure B

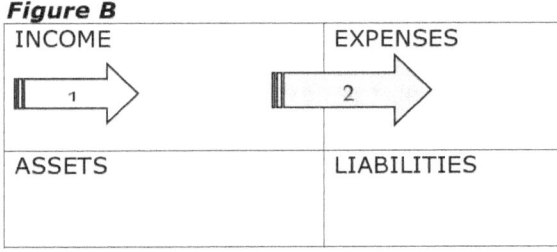

The Spending rule, or The Money-In-Money-Out rule is a rule applied by many people all over the world. It is fuelled by many different needs, wants, and beliefs about money. Marketers are working hard to get people to apply this rule through advertising and promotions. Politicians want people to spend in order to "boost" the economy. As popular as the Spending rule or money-in-money-out rule is, unfortunately, for some people, that is where they get stuck. That is the only rule they ever learn. They know that when money comes in, money must go out.

If this is the only money rule you know, it does not matter how much money is coming in. As much as comes in, must go out.

Not Enough!

The trouble with the Spending rule is that man is a growing being with growing needs and desires. As he gets used to spending for stuff, he desires more and more stuff. The trouble is that the income is not growing at the same pace with desires.

You are now experiencing the "not-enough-ness" of money. This creates a problem. Since we are natural problem solvers, we look around us to see how other people have solved this problem, and we start to emulate them.

We learn the next rule of money. Our intention is not to get into trouble, but to solve the problem of "not-enough-ness" or the problem of lack.

3. Borrowing for consumption rule

We now start to involve Other People's Money (OPM) in our money game. We look at the field and say, which quadrant has idle money? Low and behold, another player on the field, the lender, has already spotted you, and offers to solve your problem. This seems very harmless. Besides, many other fellow players on the field have utilized this strategy of solving the problem of not-enough-ness.

This is the rule that includes the next quadrant in your money field. The focus of the Borrowing-For-Consumption rule is intended to increase your income so that you can effectively carry out the Spending rule or the Money-In-Money-Out rule. You go to the lender, you fill out the forms and the next day your lender calls you and says, 'your loan has been approved'.
If you are like most people, you get excited because it seems your income has grown overnight, and now you can afford the things you couldn't afford the day before.
It is represented by the arrow (3) moving

from the liabilities quadrant to the income quadrant in the field in figure C.

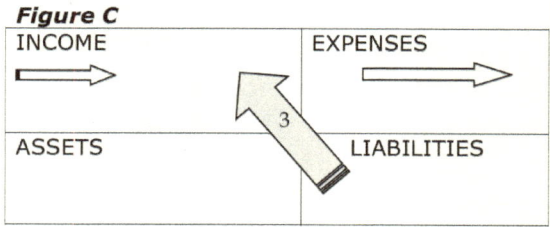

You have just temporarily increased your income by borrowing.

By the way, your lender told you that you are special. To qualify for this rule in the formal sector, it is imperative that you have an income – a salary. Many people get very excited when they are told that now they "qualify" to apply this money rule in their game.

Not everyone can apply this rule in their money game, at least not in the formal sector, although many people apply it informally, and the consequences are almost the same as in the formal sector, if not worse. When the lender calls and says you now qualify for a loan, it's as if you have achieved a milestone in your life.

This Borrowing-For-Consumption rule comes in various forms. Generally, it's in the form of a personal loan, a credit card, an overdraft facility, or a store card, or even hard cash from the lender in the form of a cash loan.

Before you introduced this rule in your life, you were pretty much playing the money game by your own money and your own rules to some extent. As soon as you learn and apply the Borrowing-For-Consumption rule, you are involving other people or entities in your money game, and they too come with their own rules, which you must now accommodate in your life. This is when you find out the next rule:

4 The Repayment Rule

All money borrowed must be repaid! This rule introduces new movement of money on your field. While you were filling in the forms at your lender's office, they informed you about this new rule, but you did not hear them, – well, you heard them but it did not register. What was important to you at the time was getting more money.

To qualify for the Borrowing-For-Consumption rule, you must prove that you are able to apply its companion rule, the Repayment rule. That is why qualifying for a loan or a credit card seems to be such an achievement for many people.

Of course, the Repayment rule does not come into play until a month or in some cases, even three months later. So, you don't feel its impact until the time to apply it comes in.

All loans create expenses through interest, and of course the repayment of the principal. On the field below (figure D) it is represented by arrow (4), which indicates a new expense that supports or feeds the liability.

Figure D

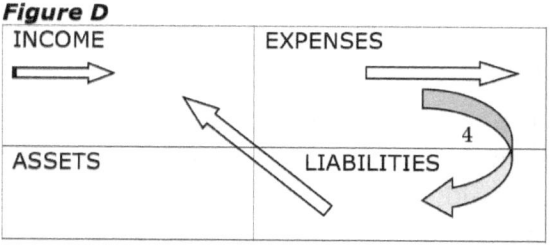

By the time of the application of the Repayment rule, you start to realise that really, your income alone is not enough. Here, a lot of people get stuck. They have learned only four money rules and they

think that's all there is to the game of money. They get stuck in a cycle.
- Money in, money out; not enough, borrow, and repay!

This is a new song that many people sing all the way to the grave.

"Money in, money out, not enough, borrow, and repay!"

The repetition is based on the fact that people don't take one loan and learn from it. They take one loan, then another, then another, without realising that they are not making any progress on their money game. They are repeating the same move over and over again. They even take loans to repay loans!

This is like the treadmill at the gym. You are running and you are getting tired but you are going nowhere. Many people spend a lifetime playing the money game by only these few limited rules. This does not apply to individuals only. Many companies, of course run by individuals who only understand these few rules, run their companies like they run their lives. Money is going out faster than it is coming in.

At this stage many people try to introduce other financial tools to try to help them. The only problem is that even these financial tools are not properly understood and so their applications seem fruitless. One of the first financial tools often applied is a tool called a Budget.

5. The Budget rule or the "spending sheet" rule

This rule at this stage should be called the Misapplied-Budget rule, or more aptly, The Spending-Sheet-Rule.
While a budget can be a truly freeing financial tool, when it is misapplied, it becomes a very restricting tool and many people don't like it.

We use a 'budget' to try to reduce our spending and to restrict our life-styles. What we call a budget is really a Spending Sheet.
At the end of every month we look at what remains of our income after everyone else, including the government, have taken their share, and we draw up a sheet that will determine what we should do with the balance.
It's like you have cooked this pot of food, dished out for everyone else, and now you

have to live on the leftovers, if any.

We notice that money is going out faster than it is coming in and we are seeking to plug the holes of the apparently sinking ship, but we can't seem to be able to bail the water out fast enough. This Budget that was supposed to help me is only serving to restrict me and limit me. I am not happy.

We are freedom-seeking beings and we don't like it when our lives are restricted. The nature of a human being is to seek expression, not restriction.

After a while of budgeting and fidgeting, and getting frustrated, we toss the budget out because as far as we are concerned, it does not work. Most of us return to the rules we know, including the borrowing for consumption rule, and we continue to sing the same old song we have sung before!

This game seems to be unwinnable! There is an underlying problem in this money game.

What is it? What is it? (The budget rule has no representation on the money field since it's just about organisation and planning, and not moving money).

SELF-ASSESSMENT

1. Name and give a brief description of each of the five money rules learnt thus far in this chapter.
2. How does "not-enough-ness" affect your money game?
3. What is the "song" sung by most people that are stuck in the money game?

Chapter 6

6. MORE PLAYERS ON THE MONEY FIELD

"Financial peace isn't the acquisition of stuff. It's learning to live on less than you make, so you can give money back and have money to invest. You can't win until you do this."
Dave Ramsey

LEARNING OUTCOMES
In this chapter you will learn:
- Why saving seems fruitless
- The borrowing for asset rule
- The repossession and the surrender rule

We have been introduced to the money field

and have started to notice how easy it is to formulate money habits. We just allow money to come and go without some apparent controls on our part. We have seen the weakness of our problem-solving systems. Let us continue to see some of the things we do on the money field.

As you get along in years, you realise that you really can't live like this any longer. You have to find something that will help you. This is when you really start thinking about the next rule in the money game:

6. The Savings Rule

You have always known about savings and how important they are. In fact, your salary may even be received into a so-called Savings Account. The only problem with this so-called savings account is that it comes with an ATM (Automated Teller Machine) card that also has buying capabilities.

Whatever you have put in that account, every time you see an ATM, it seems to have a magnetic ability to draw you to it, and it makes you withdraw money. Every time you enter a store, there is a swiping machine there for your convenience.

I think this account should be called a Spending Account. After all, that's all it ever seems to be able to do for you.

Now you start to realise that you have to have either a separate real savings account where you can put something aside, or devise some other means of saving money.

You make a decision to save money. But, to save money, something has to give. You either have to cut back on some of your expenses, get out of debt, or find a way to generate more income.

Finally, you decide to join a savings club, a Stokvel or "motshelo", where every month the members commit to put something aside as a saving. Or you just go to your bank and open a savings account.

This introduces a new route on your money field. For the first time, something starts going into your Asset quadrant.

This is indicated by arrow (5) in your money field (Figure E).

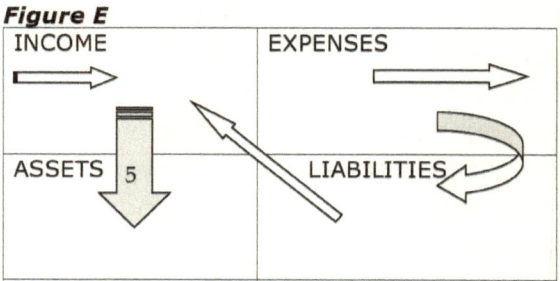

Figure E

Saving money takes many forms for many of us. There is long-term savings and short-term savings. For many of us, long-term savings, even though we may participate in them, are far removed from us and it therefore seems that they do not exist because we don't see the money.

This is the pension or retirement fund that gets deducted from our salary before we see it. Some of us have taken a life insurance policy or an insurance savings policy. These long-term products don't always play on the field in our daily money game.

The visible savings-rule comes into play when we are saving for a particular thing in our lives like a piece of furniture, a vehicle, or a holiday.

There are other forms of savings that we engage in.

Some are formal through financial

institutions, and others are on a more informal fashion as mentioned above. These include social programs such as what we call Stokvel or "Motshelo".

Under these social savings programs, a group of us gather together on a monthly basis and we put a certain agreed amount into a fund. This fund is usually put into a savings account and our commitment is that each member should contribute every month.

The operation of these programs has evolved over time. In their original fashion, they were for saving for a whole year and then dividing up the money at the end of the year and starting over again the following year. The evolution of these funds now includes lending money to their members over the year and charging them an interest. This is meant to increase the fund so that at the end of the year there is more to divide among the members.

There is no real advantage when only members borrow and charge themselves interest. The real advantage is when these funds lend to non-members and charge them interest. In this way the members of the fund will benefit from the outside source of income, which serves to increase each member's share at the end of the year.

Regulators are constantly watching to make sure that these social schemes don't turn into loan sharks as well.

They seek to restrict the lending and borrowing action to happen only among the members.

Since many people stuck in the life-style debt cycle as shown in the previous chapter, many members come back to these funds to continue their borrowing life cycle, and may be unable to repay, and at the end of the year, they would really have nothing left in the fund. The money-in-money-out system is very strong.

7. The Return of savings rule

With the Savings-Rule we come to realise that there is another rule at work called, Money-Saved-Comes-Back rule, or simply, the Return on Savings.

This, as we mentioned, may be at the end of the year when the fund is divided among members, or when a savings policy matures.

This introduces new flow on the money field and is indicated by arrow (6) in the money field below (Figure F).

Figure F

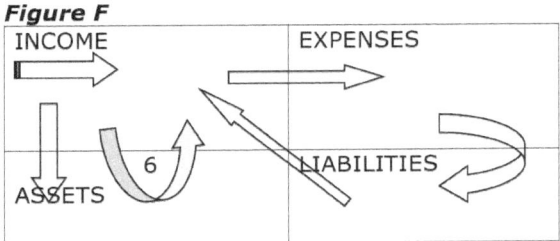

This is money from your assets - (a savings account or fund) - into your income quadrant.
When money comes back to you from your savings, what you do with it depends on your psychology of money, and how the other rules are playing on your money field.
For most of us, as soon as money comes back into our income quadrant, the first rule automatically kicks in: Spend!

8. The Money-In-Money-Out rule.

The old habits kick in, we continue with our old life pattern and money rules. This is indicated by arrow (7) in the field below (Figure G).

Figure G

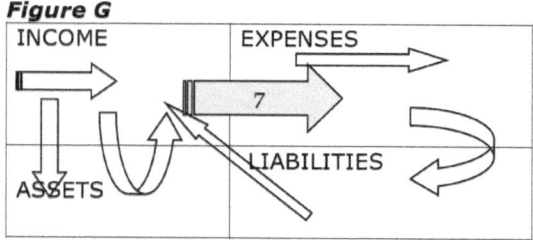

As you can see, arrow 7 is not really a new movement of money on the money field. It is just a repetition of the old Money-in-money-out rule. This can be a very frustrating time for many of us.

We have played just about all the money rules we know in the money game, but still, we are going nowhere.

We have worked for years, we have tried to budget, we have borrowed, we have saved, but we are still going nowhere. We accept this as how life is.

At this stage we have already formed many beliefs about money because of our experience. We know what works and what doesn't work, generally, we seem to know that nothing works.

How then does anyone get anywhere in this life? At this stage, beliefs like, "You can't live without debt" are cemented. You are getting along in years. The game doesn't stop. It must go on. You have been working for many years now. You have earned many salaries over the years but you still feel like you have nothing to show for it. You need to have at least a house of your own. A new rule must come into play on your money field.

9. The Borrow-For-Assets rule

You feel the need to own a real asset. Your own salary is never going to do it, so you do what everyone is doing. You go down to your local bank to apply for your first mortgage. Since you are still gainfully employed, and your rental can now be diverted to your mortgage, you qualify, and the new rule comes into play.

The borrowing for asset rule is a variation of the borrowing for consumption rule. The difference is that when you borrow for consumption, it is often in the form of unsecured loans, credit cards, or store cards, whereas, when you borrow for an asset like a house or a piece of immovable property, you have something more tangible to show for your loan.

This is the Borrow-for-Asset rule and the field starts to look like this, with the new rule represented by arrow (8) on the field (Figure H):

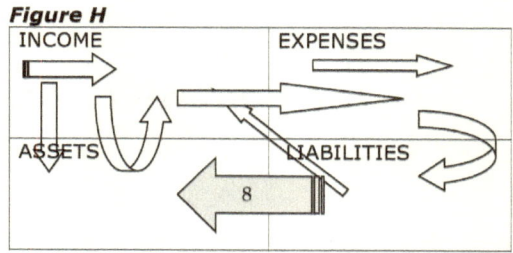

However, just like the Borrow-For-consumption rule, the Borrow-for-Asset rule works hand in hand with the Money-Borrowed-Must-Be-Repaid rule. For most of us, our overcommitted salary remains responsible for the repayment of this loan. Every loan creates an expense.

As the repayment rule kicks into play, the field looks like this, with the new repayment represented by arrow (9) on the field (Figure I):

Figure I

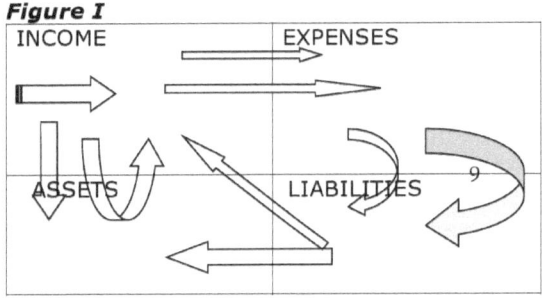

As you can see, arrow number 9 is not new. It is a repetition of the old repayment rule. All money borrowed must be repaid. We've been here before. Are we making progress or going around in circles? As you can see, it's crowded on the money field. There are arrows going every which way. Many people go through life with this kind of money field. And this is called normal life. Based on this kind of money field, we build our beliefs about life. Millions of people live in the financial red line.

Many people reach retirement living from pay-cheque to pay-cheque, and they are forced now to live according to their 'budgets' because now they have no more strength to keep earning money to continue these rules on the money field.

In a worst-case scenario, other people get to experience other rules on the field.

Another rule that other people get to experience in their lives, and more and more on an increasing scale, is the repossession rule.

10. The Repossession Rule

This rule is born of the Money-Borrowed-Must-Be-Repaid rule. Anyone who fails to obey the Repayment rule gets to experience the Repossession rule.

The repossession rule of course means that "your assets" go back to your creditors. This is represented by arrow (10) in the money field (Figure J)

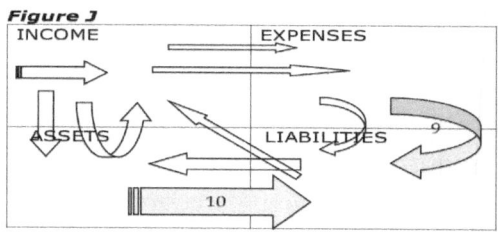

Some of us, realising where we are, and being unable to move on, we apply another rule called the Surrender rule.

11. The Surrender Rule

The surrender rule is when we start selling off our own assets just to try to increase our income to live on. The flow on the money field is the same as with the Repossession Rule.

In both cases, assets are leaving our assets quadrant.

When money leaves our asset quadrant, our net worth goes down, all in an attempt to increase our income.

Now the entire field of play looks like this (Figure K):

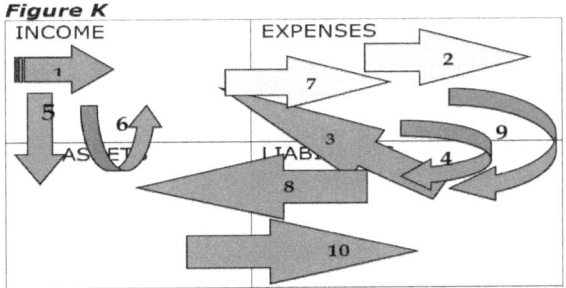

Figure K

All the arrows from 1 to 10 represented.
1. The Earning Rule
2. The Spending Rule
3. The Borrowing for Consumption Rule
4. The Repayment Rule

5. The Savings Rule
6. The Return on Savings Rule
7. The Spending Rule (again)
8. The Borrowing for Assets Rule
9. The Repayment Rule (again)
10. The Repossession or Surrender Rule

This is the bleeding money field. Many people live in the financial red line. In the next chapter, we will focus on a different money field.

What could we do if we played this game intelligently? What are the different moves that the financially intelligent people do on the money field?

SELF-ASSESSMENT

1. Name and give a brief description of each of the Money Rules learnt in this chapter thus far.
2. What is the benefit of borrowing for assets?
3. How do the Repossession rule and the Surrender rule differ or overlap?

Chapter 7

7. THE VALUE OF AN INCOME

"It's not the employer who pays the wages. Employers only handle the money. It's the customer who pays the wages."
Henry Ford

LEARNING OUTCOMES
In this chapter you will learn:
- The value of an income
- Pay yourself first

People who play the money game intelligently seem to be playing by a completely different set of rules. In this chapter I would like you to consider the rules that can be helpful in winning the game.
Some of them, you may already be convinced that they don't work, but perhaps

considering a new way of applying old rules can bring different results.
Before we look at the money field specifically and to understand the new rules, let us consider some things that are very important.

1. The Value of an Income

The wise have observed that often you don't value something until you lose it. Anyone who's ever lost a job knows the value of a job.

A job is the way most people make their living. However, increasingly we see that as the world population increases, shrinking industries can't keep up with the demands for new jobs, and therefore more and more people stay unemployed. This must lead to the rise of entrepreneurship, because whether employed or not, people will still demand goods and services. To be able to be an effective player in the money game, it is important that one has an income. An income is not only as a result of a job, but any commercially viable activity. An income creates possibilities.

If you have a source of income, it is

important to value it, and not waste it. Stay positive, work with what you have and then enter the field.

We all start at the same point, whether financially literate or not. We start with an income whether from a job or from entrepreneurship, or as gift or inheritance. As was illustrated before, it is represented by the first arrow (1) in the field (Figure L).

Figure L

INCOME ⟶ 1	EXPENSES
ASSETS	LIABILITIES

For most people, when money comes into their money field, it creates emotions.

If left unchecked, these emotions will give direction to the money. The question would be, what would a financially intelligent person do when they receive money?

2. Who takes my money before I do?

Before we introduce the first rule of a financially literate person, let us honestly consider the following questions and their answers:

1. How often do you pay your landlord or mortgage company? (Every month?)
2. How often do you pay your electricity company? (Monthly?)
3. How often do you pay your water company? (Monthly?)
4. How often do you pay your telephone company?
    a. Your cellular phone company?
    b. Your land-line company?
    c. Your Internet service provider?
5. How often do you pay your grocery store?
6. How often do you pay your fuel station?

It is obvious to all of us that these are the

institutions or people we pay on a very regular basis. They seem to be the providers of our most basic needs, and therefore seem to deserve our money. When money comes in, we think of them first.

Is that how a financially intelligent person should think? What options do they have? Well, the financially intelligent start with a different question. Let us pose this question to you and see what your answer is:

3. How often do you pay yourself?

What is your honest answer to that question?

"Pay myself? How can I pay myself?" That is the most frequent answer I get when I ask that question.

Most people are stunned by this question, because they assume that just because the salary comes in their name, it is theirs. And yet they pass it on to everybody else, and they are left with nothing.

Or, they pay everybody else, and whatever remains, if any, they get to keep. This is the exact mentality that keeps people in the financial red line. Another frequent answer to the question is: "I pay myself when I spoil myself!"

I ask, what do you mean by spoiling yourself?

"I take myself out to fancy restaurants, or buy myself nice things that make me happy"

I ask, how much money comes to you when you do that?

Then they realise, money doesn't come to me, it leaves me, but it leaves me happy, they argue. Then I ask, if it left you, did you pay yourself, or did you pay someone else?

Who Else Takes Your Money Before You Do?

Are there predators on your money's path? From your employer or your clients to you, who has access to it before you do?

Have you set up systems to allow people access to your money?

Not everyone who has access to your money before you do is a predator. Some are good guys like your Retirement contribution, because that's still money belonging to you.

Some are of course predators that once they have your money, you will never see it again.

Even if you have cash in your hand,

consider that when you deposit it in an account, there will be a predator called, 'cash deposit fee'. If you withdraw money, there is 'withdrawal fee'. (Don't forget about these little invisible guys) So list the beneficiaries and the predators on your money's path. Look at your pay slip and you will know.

Discomfort in The Presence of Cash?

Most people are cash avoiders! Have you noticed that about yourself? You might say, how can I be a cash avoider?

It sounds silly, doesn't it? But yes, most people are against cash, that's why they'd rather spend it.

Have you noticed that the institutions and people we listed above wants cash but you? They demand cash from you, and that is why you pay them first.

You, however, seem to prefer stuff. As soon as you hold cash in your hands, you want to exchange it for 'stuff'.

You are eager to get rid of it. When you have cash, you can't sit still. You want to go out and spend it. That is what we mean by saying that you hate cash.

Many people are literally uncomfortable in the presence of cash. By getting rid of cash you are getting rid of the tools you need to play the money game.

Cash is the most important tool in the money game. To play the game, you need to have cash. Without cash, you can't play the game. Some try to play with borrowed money, but as we have seen, borrowed money plays by its own rules. To effectively play this game you need to practice the first rule of money. In the next chapter, we will look at the first rule of a financially intelligent person.

SELF-ASSESSMENT
1. What does it mean that people take your money before you do?
2. Who takes your money before you do?
3. What does it mean to pay yourself first?
4. What does it mean to be uncomfortable in the presence of cash?
5. What is the value of an income?

The Money Field book series – 3-in-1

Chapter 8

8. CONSUMER BEHAVIOUR

"It is your "Attitude", not your "aptitude", that will determine your "Altitude"!"
Zig Ziegler

LEARNING OUTCOMES
- Important questions about consumers
- The commercialisation of our senses
- How to restore functional literacy

Why do the ordinary people play the money game the way that they do? Who taught them to play that way? Who said to them, as soon as you receive your money, you must spend it in a hurry.

Who said to them, if you run out of money, you should just borrow it. How come people borrow money and seem to stay disconnected from the fact that they have to repay way more than they borrowed? Why is it that most people don't see the addictive trap of borrowed money?

How come they find themselves ensnared until it's too late? Why do they think they can get out of debt by borrowing more money?

Who said to them that debt consolidation or debt restructuring is equivalent to debt management?

Who sawed these seeds of confusion?

If we can all sit down and begin to answer all of these questions, perhaps we can begin to understand consumer behaviour. Let us take a moment to understand ourselves. How do the other players influence our personal money game on the money field?

The Commercialization of Our Senses

The senses. All five of them. Given to humanity to navigate rugged planet earth. Before we evolved, they were larger than life. Big ears, big eyes, big hands, open nostrils and a rough tongue to handle uncooked diet. Then we evolved.

Being presentable was redefined and beauty took over. Make-up for the eyes, nose jobs, hair to cover large ears, manicure, pedicure, and creams for the soft touch effects, and redefined job for the tongue. We may have forgotten our origins and the power of our senses, but commerce never forgot.

We are still largely motivated by our senses. They get us to act without much thinking. More often than not, our senses overcome our thoughts. You have a well-constructed, well thought out budget plan, but when you enter the shopping mall, your senses take over the shopping experience, and out goes your budget plan.

Any shopping mall you enter, there is a call to one or more of your senses. Your ears pick up sound waves of music that remind you of way back when … and a desire to acquire that piece is activated, for posterity, of course! Mind you, the entire music industry would not exist if you did not have ears!

The perfume shop around the corner assaults your sense of smell and remind you of your lover, while the aroma from the food court activates hunger pangs that were otherwise asleep. Without your nose, the whole perfume industry would not exist.

The seemingly invisible blended colours make the mall seem natural while they activate the buying instincts within you. If you did not have eyes, colour would not matter.

The mood is just right, the music soft and appealing, the air filled with the scent of newness. You are invited by the sales person to just try it on, or just touch, which activates your sense of touch and make you feel good. You couldn't possibly put it down, could you?

The sales person might think you are broke, and we wouldn't want them thinking that now, would we? Out comes the credit card and whoosh! Impulsive buying has been activated. Who can stop it now?

Finally, you succumb to the hunger and you sit down to feast your eyes on the colourful menu that gets you to salivate even before you order your food. Of course, there are unplanned starters to get you started. Would you like to pre-order your desert? It's Crème brûlée! Before you know it, you are full and you are asking for the doggie bag to make room for the desert! Why did you ever order so much food when you were really not that hungry? Who is in charge? Your mind or your senses? Do you think or do you feel?

The goal of commercialization is to get you to feel more; to follow your senses; to forget about your thoughts. Let the chemicals flow in your veins! Only afterwards, when the bill from the credit card company comes, do you plead with your head to think of a plan to get you out! Again, we ask, who is in charge here?

Functional Literacy

Functional ***illiteracy*** is high even in first world countries that have a 100% literacy rates. According to the Barbara Bush Foundation for Family Literacy[6], fully 27% of all American adults are "<u>functionally illiterate</u>".

In simple terms, this means, if supermarkets were to close down, these people would not know what to do to survive. That is functional illiteracy. Financial literacy is one of the pillars that

---

[6] Hartmann Thom, *The Last Hours of Ancient Sunlight*, Three Rivers Press, NY, 2004

can promote functional literacy.

The management of personal finances is vital in creating solid citizens who are in turn able to manage not only their own affairs, but the affairs of corporations, NGO's and government departments.

When managers are unable to manage their own personal affairs, they cannot realistically be expected to manage the affairs of corporations and organisations.

We have also come to realize that in addition to functional and financial strategies that are missing, one of the greatest contributing factors to financial illiteracy is the dysfunctional psychology of money.

Life skills and coping strategies are some of the things that can increase functional literacy. The promotion of emotional intelligence can build stable societies that are able to solve day-to-day problems and be able to project future solutions.

Functional behaviour is that which allows an individual to prosper in life by:

- Setting personal and financial goals
- Functionally "living in the gap" and moving towards meeting financial goals

- Behaving in a way that supports their financial goals and values
- Upholding functional and supportive money beliefs
- Keeping good personal financial records
- Being well informed in order to take appropriate financial decisions at critical times
- Being financially protected and not vulnerable to immitigable risks
- Keeping healthy relationships with other people in relation to money
- Living within and expanding their means
- Building a healthy nest egg for retirement

SELF-ASSESSMENT

1. Which industries depend on which parts of our senses?
2. How can consumers be more aware of how their senses are being commercialised?
3. What is functional illiteracy?
4. How can financial literacy improve functional illiteracy?

The Intelligent Money Field

Nelson Letshwene

Chapter 9

9. THE INTELLIGENT MONEY FIELD

"If you don't change direction, you may end up where you are heading"
Lao Tzu.

> LEARNING OUTCOMES
> In this chapter you will learn:
> - How the wealthy apply money rules on the money field
> - The importance of the Pay Yourself First rule
> - The Balanced Split Rule
> - The Spider Web Economic doctrine

How do financially intelligent people play their money game? What are the most important rules that they follow? How do they keep their emotions in check? Who do they choose to involve in their money game? Who do they avoid on the money field? Who is in their team? What does it take to be a financially intelligent player?

1. The Pay Yourself First Rule

The Pay-Yourself-First rule is the most important rule in building financial stability. The application of this rule is the first step in the right direction, regardless of where you are in your life right now.

Even if you are currently living in the financial red line, your hope of escape is the Pay-Yourself-First rule. This rule starts to change the direction of money. Instead of starting with expenses, you start with your assets. This is represented by arrow (2) in the field below (Figure M):

Figure M

INCOME	EXPENSES
ASSETS	LIABILITIES

The Pay Yourself First rule was popularized

by George Clason in his 1926 classic, *The Richest Man In Babylon*. In the book, the richest man teaches his students this rule:

> "A part of all you earn is yours to keep!"

His idea is that whatever money comes to you from whatever source, you must keep some for yourself! You must start building your asset base! He reckons your target should be 10%.

Until you learn <u>to keep</u> money, you have no hope of employing money for growth. You can't gainfully employ someone else's money. It can only work for them. You must learn to keep and employ your own.

How Do You Pay Yourself First?

Many people look at what they earn and how much they have to spend and they immediately know the answer to that question. It is impossible! How can I pay myself first when what I have is not even enough for me to live on? That is indeed a very important question and it will be answered later on as the pages roll on.

But the quick answer is that the reason for instituting the pay yourself first rule now is to try to create a new habit in your life. Many of us do not have the right habits when it comes to dealing with money.

Now, without worrying about the amount right now, ask yourself: have you established a savings habit? If not, this is the main reason for this rule.

George Clason recommends 10% of all that comes to you. Even if you can't afford 10% right now, you need to institute a habit of saving, with 10% as your target. Work at it until you are able to save at least 10%, and then work to increase that if you can.

Consider the idea that your current money habits may not be helping you, and you need to start new habits, one at a time.

For most of us, the only source of income that we have is our employment.

The Pay-Yourself-First rule introduces the concept of employing a resource called money, and this rule brings into play the Money-Saved-Comes-Back rule that we looked at earlier.

In the next chapter we will focusing or dealing with some of the obstacles to saving.

2. The Return on Investments (ROI) Rule

Saved money has a potential to earn you more money in the form of interest. If invested well, it can also bring back dividends and profits.

You will never earn interest, dividends, or profits until you learn to pay yourself first.

On the money field (figure N), this is indicated by arrow (3), money coming back into your income quadrant from your asset quadrant.

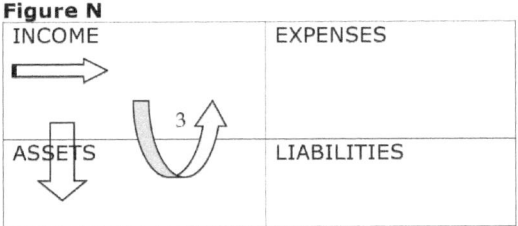

Money saved comes back in its totality as well as in the form of interest or other forms of returns on investments (ROI).

In other words, money saved in a proper way never comes back alone. The principal always comes back with a return. I'm not talking about speculative investments.

It is important to take the Pay-yourself-first

rule seriously because in it lies the hope of success. This rule, although a natural rule of increase, is unknown or disregarded by a lot of people.

If you have not yet read George Clason's *The Richest Man in Babylon,* I recommend that you read it to begin to build some financial literacy.
In that book are some rules of money that are very helpful in building financial intelligence.
How does a Financially Intelligent person utilise their money?

3. The Balanced Split Rule

The Balanced Split rule says, when money comes in, instead of immediately applying the Money-in-Money-Out rule, rather think about some money staying in your income quadrant, some going to the Asset quadrant, and some going to your expenses quadrant.
If you learn to keep just 10% of your earnings, 90% remains for you to play your expense game.

The balanced split is represented by arrow (4) in the money field (Figure O). The arrow shows money going into the expenses quadrant, some going into the asset quadrant, and some staying in the income quadrant.

Figure O

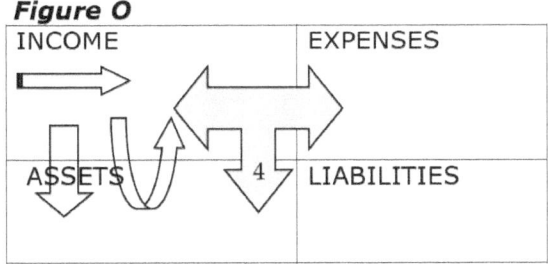

There is a psychological trick to never being broke, that is, always having money in your income quadrant. Don't allow yourself to go broke. Create a habit of always having money on your person.

If you are used to the application of the Money-in-Money-out rule, this may be strange and difficult at first, but it is the way to think about money effectively.

The classic statement in *The Richest Man in Babylon,* when personalized, says, "a part of all I earn is mine to keep". Are you a keeper or a spender? When do I start the Balanced Split rule? The answer is NOW! Some say, but my current system does not allow me any amount of money to be saved now.

I say, if going forward is what you would like to see happen in your life, then perhaps you should change your systems and make sure that you put yourself first. This may mean putting some that used to be first, last. This does not suggest being irresponsible, but it means adjusting and adapting.

4. The Spider-Web Economic Doctrine

Chika Onyeani, in his book, *Capitalist Nigger – The road to success*, introduces something he calls the spider-web economic doctrine applied by Asians in America to gain economic freedom. They create business networks such that all money that comes into such a network, never leaves the network. They build businesses of everything they need. Outsiders come and buy from them, but they never go and buy from outsiders.

They only spend their money within the network of businesses owned by one of them. This ensures that even their expenses, will come back as an income as whoever they bought from, will also come and buy from them. They understand the balanced split rule. They spend with ease because they have set up systems to ensure that the money they spend will come back to them as an income.

> The spider web:
> The network is made up of connected individuals and entities that seek to support each other. When the owner of shop 1 wants an item, like clothing, they only buy from shop 2, and when the owner of shop 2 wants a car, they go to shop 3, who goes to shop 4 for some other item, etc. They allow outsiders to come and shop from them, but no one in the web buys anything outside this circle. This ensures that their money stays with the group, which forms a cartel.

SELF-ASSESSMENT

1. Explain the Pay-yourself-first rule
2. What is the spider-web economic doctrine?
3. Explain the balanced split rule
4. What are the benefits of paying yourself first?

Chapter 10

10. WHY IS IT DIFFICULT TO SAVE MONEY?

"There is nothing we receive with so much reluctance as advice."
Joseph Addison.

> LEARNING OUTCOMES
> In this chapter you will learn:
> 1. What makes savings so difficult
> 2. Problems related to lack of savings
> 3. Creating reasons for saving

The argument says, but saving doesn't work, I've done it for so many years and still I get to spend the money I have saved, I still have nothing to help me now, I have nothing to show for all my savings. It's one step forward, and two steps backwards.

Do you want to change? Would you like to

effectively apply the Balanced Split rule?

George Clason said it best: a part of all I earn is mine to keep. The keeping principle has been at the root of building wealth since money was invented.

It is only those that are able to keep money that are capacitated to build wealth. It does not matter how much you make, it matters how much you keep.

Those that are expert money spenders do not have a hope of building wealth. The worst are those who play the money game with other people's money, that is, borrowed money.

What are the reasons that many people can't practice the keeping principle? Many people's financial lives are unstructured. Everything is a surprise and therefore everything is an emergency. There is no forward thinking and there is no plan that is being followed. Even things that should not be a surprise are always a surprise including school fees and birthdays; and some people are in the habit of solving such "emergencies" by taking a loan, which creates other obvious problems of living for your creditors.

5. The Anti-Saving Obstacles

So, some of the problems are:
- *Lack of structure* in your finances will prevent you from being able to practice the keeping principle.
- *Lack of purpose or "reason why".* Purpose creates motivation. Without a strong enough "Why", most people never save! This means setting goals and targets for saving.
  Saving money for no particular reason is not a good way to practice the keeping principle. You need to create a strong reason and motivation for saving.
- *Lack of proper financial planning.* Without a plan, you are shooting into the dark.
- *Ignorance of proper financial tools and instruments* that you can use to catapult you into a wealth builder.
  - ➢ If you choose to use the *stock market* as your tool, you must be informed of its intricacies so that you can derive maximum benefit from your efforts.
  - ➢ If you choose to use *real estate* as

> your tool, you have to know a lot about that sector.
> ➢ If you choose *business*, you cannot be a scatterbrain that runs from business idea to business idea.

- *Sabotaging yourself* includes what we call stealing from yourself. You save for a particular purpose, like, to put down a deposit for a house, and then you divert the money to buy a car or to some other project unrelated to your initial purpose. That is self-sabotage. You are what Walt Kelly's cartoon character Pogo meant when he said: "we have met the enemy, and he is us!"
- *Planning and not following your plan*. They say if you fail to plan, you have planned to fail. But then again, if you plan and do not follow through, you have also planned to fail.
- And of course, there are a lot of *disempowering beliefs* that make you think it is impossible to build wealth through savings! Check your beliefs.

The enemy could be right inside. It is time to change your mind about your capabilities!

The maxim from here on should be, "when money comes in, 'I will keep some and I will spend some'; or, 'a part of all I earn is mine to keep'.

For those who say, 'but I don't earn enough to save', I say, at this stage, it is not so much about how much you save, the most important thing is to start the habit of saving.

It is at this stage that some say: save for what? I can't save money when I have very little to live on!

6. Purposeful Saving

The fact is, all purposeless saving will eventually disappear. If you save money but you have not assigned a specific task for it, some emergency will come and take it away.

- Find a purpose for your money, that is the only way you can keep it.
- Saving for an investment.
- Save it because you want some returns to come back to you.
- Save it because you want it to start

working for you.
- Save it to start the new habit of saving. Our habits imprison us and the sooner we break the shackles off our feet, the sooner we can walk freely.

Savings have proved to be difficult for many of us because we see a saving as a thing that keeps you from enjoying your money. We also see saving as an end in itself instead of a means to an end.

The end is ROI (return on investments), not savings. When you save aimlessly, any pressure that comes will utilise your savings. But when you save with intent to invest, especially if that investment is important to you, then nothing will dissuade you from your path.

If you are saving money for a deposit on a house, then saving does not seem so difficult. If you are saving, just so that you can have money if an emergency comes, then the emergency almost always comes. All aimless savings end up nowhere. All purposeful savings lead to goal achievement. The application of the pay-yourself-first rule must be with intent to invest into some important project that will in turn produce satisfactory results for you.

The most important thing is to start the habit of saving!

SELF-ASSESSMENT

1. What has made saving money difficult? (list at least five reasons)
2. What are the good and viable reasons for saving money?
3. How can you start and sustain the habit of saving?

Nelson Letshwene

Chapter 11

11. DEBT AND FINANCIAL INTELLIGENCE

"I've been rich, and I've been poor; now that I know which is which, I'd rather be rich."
Dan Lee Dimke

> LEARNING OUTCOMES
>
> In this chapter you will learn:
> - How the financially intelligent borrow money
> - New conditions for borrowing money
> - The performing assets rule
> - The sponsoring rule
>
> Creating Security

Financial intelligence is not the domain of the rich only. Anyone who is willing to engage the rules, can benefit from all quadrants of the money game.

7. Do Financially Intelligent People Borrow Money?

A financially intelligent person does borrow money; but when she does, she makes sure of a few things. First, she does not borrow excessively for consumption, and if she can help it, she does not borrow for consumption at all.

When she does borrow for consumption, for example, as in credit card, she makes sure that she does not carry a balance on her credit card. This means whatever she charged on her credit card this month, gets paid off at the end of the month. Credit card companies only charge you interest on the balance left unpaid at the end of the month on your credit card. If you pay off everything you charged, you are essentially using their money for free.

Your reasons or motivation for borrowing money will go a long way in telling you about your relationship with your money, and other people's money. A financially intelligent person does not, as a general rule, borrow money without a full plan and debt strategy. She does not borrow money out of panic. She does not borrow money "for problems". She does not borrow money to repay debt.

If you say, okay, but I've made some financial mistakes. For example, I'm carrying a balance on my credit card, what do I do now? That's a good question.

This whole book works as a unit. The section on Debt management systems will come in handy.

The key is to remain calm and not panic because it is very difficult to counsel panic. A person who is drowning tends to panic, but it is precisely remaining calm that could save that person's life. If you feel that you are drowning in debt, being calm right now may lead you to the most amicable solutions.

This is better than the irrational application of more debt to cover debt, thus perpetuating the problem.

8. Borrowing for Security

Let us address one of the most important concepts when it comes to borrowing money. Among the many advices that the richest man gave to his students in George Clason's *The Richest Man in Babylon* was this:

"make of thy dwelling a profitable investment"

Many a man spends too many years of their working life paying exorbitant rentals to landlords. It is easy to think that it is cheaper to rent than to own. But because you are essentially losing time, in the long run, it proves to be more expensive to rent than to own. All that money that has gone to the landlord for all these years, could have gone towards the repayment of your own home loan.

It makes sense to buy or build your own home as a matter of priority. Creating security for yourself and your family is the first step towards freedom.

If you are going to borrow money, you can borrow for your home.

What does not make sense, however, is to spend twenty-five to thirty years paying for your first home. Yes, the lender said you can take up to thirty years to repay your mortgage. But don't forget that lenders are also players on the money field. The longer you take to repay this loan the more money they make off of you.

Now, think about this. If you take that long to pay off your first home loan, when do you think you will start focusing on other investments that will actually bring you an income? Your home will not bring you an income. It only gives you security. So, technically speaking, it is not an investment.

A career lasts for only forty years. If you start working at 20 to retire at 60, you only have 40 years. If you devote 30 years to paying off only one asset that will not bring in money, aren't you wasting time?

One of the things that prolongs home loan repayments are people who treat their house as if it's an ATM. They keep borrowing any extra equity from the home, reverting back to another 30 years.

The fact is, it is not impossible to pay off your home loan in 15 years or less. It does not even require that much more extra payments for you to achieve this. Look at the example below:

> Let's look at an example with numbers:
> If you borrowed one million (1'000'000), to repay it over 30 years (360 months), and you are charged say

> an interest of 11% p.a.; using a financial calculator (or formula) you will find that your monthly repayments will be equal to 9'523.23.
>
> (Now, multiply the 9'523.23 by 360 months to see the total you will repay for your one million loan. The answer is: 3'428'362.80!) This mean the lender will make an extra 2,4million off of you.
>
> [For additional shock, using the amortisation function of a financial calculator, consider that in the 9th year of this loan, that is, after 108 months of paying your instalments, you shall have paid back 1'028'508.80.to the lender. You have literally paid back the 1'000'000 and more, but you still owe a principal of 934'685.80 – upon which interest will still be charged. The Principal you shall have paid thus far is only 65'314.20. The rest of what you have paid is interest amounting to 963'194.64]
>
> Now, what if you decided to sacrifice your entertainment money and added only 280.00 per month to your monthly home loan repayment?
>
> This means your repayments will now be 9'803.23.
>
> This will save you a full five years (60 months).
>
> You will have saved 488'025.00 in interest!
>
> If you decided to repay the same mortgage over 15 years instead of 30, your repayments will only be 11'365.96.
>
> The difference between 30 years and 15 years is only 1'842.73 per month!

This is the power of compound interest. Make it work in your favour instead of against you. Any self-respecting bank will have mortgage calculators on their website. You don't need to be an accountant to calculate this. Just go that website and enter the numbers and see. By just changing your repayment amount, you will see how much time it will take you. By just changing time, you will see how much more you have to repay. You don't even have to go to the bank's website; right there on your smart phone, you can search and download any mortgage calculator App.

9. Performing Assets Rule

When a financially intelligent person borrows money, they borrow for Performing Assets. A performing asset is an asset that makes money for you. A non-performing asset is an asset that does not make you money.
Your home, for example, is a non-performing asset. But it is a very crucial part of your asset base since it gives you security.

Borrowing for Performing Assets is represented by arrow (5) in the field below (Figure P). It is money coming from lenders (liabilities) but focusing on building an asset base.

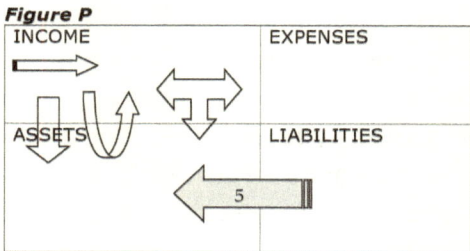
Figure P

This is the same movement that will happen when you borrow for security, that is, your primary home. Since you now know that the Repayment rule will come into play whenever you borrow money, as a financially intelligent person, you must be prepared for this.

For performing asset rule, the question financially intelligent people ask before they borrow money is: who is going to repay this loan? This will lead us to the next important consideration in the money game.

10. The Positive Cash Rule

The Positive cash rule says every time you borrow money, it must generate positive cash, as opposed to negative cash. This means setting yourself up to make money from your loans.

Financially intelligent people therefore make sure that two things will be applicable in order to fulfil the positive cash rule:

1) The asset for which the loan was taken must be the kind of asset that can generate an income. The Income must be used to repay the loan;
2) It must also generate enough income into the income quadrant so that the borrower benefits from the loan.

On the money field (Figure Q), the first rule is represented by arrow (6).

This indicates that the money that repays the loan comes from the loan itself, or that the asset is generating income.

Let's look at the first rule of financially intelligent borrowing.

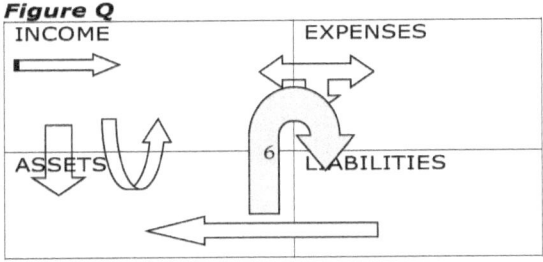

Whenever you borrow money, you make sure that you are not the one who is going to repay the loan.

An example of a performing asset for which you can borrow money and have this rule apply is real estate. If you borrowed money intelligently and purchased a rental property, that property should generate the cash to repay the loan.

11. The Profit Rule or Income from Liabilities Rule

The second rule of borrowing is to ensure that, not only is the loan generating money to repay itself, but it must also generate money for you to benefit immediately from it. This is represented on the field (Figure R) by arrow (7), showing that your income is increasing as a direct function of the loan.

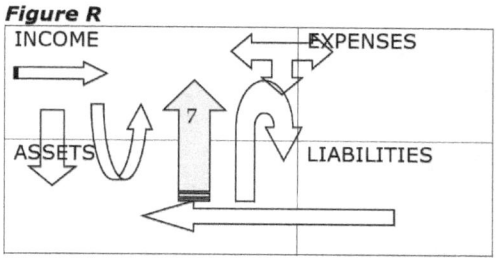

Figure R

The field below (Figure S), represents the

three arrows all together. Arrows number 5, 6, and 7 must remain inextricably combined.

A performing asset loan (5) that creates cash to repay the loan (6), and a profit (7), is an intelligent loan.
The sum of arrows 6 and 7 represent positive cash flow.

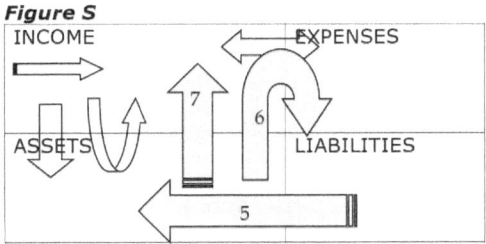
Figure S

12. The Sponsoring Rule

What most people do is they borrow money and buy a rental property. But because they don't do proper homework or understand the positive cash rule, the property becomes a burden on them.

Because the property does not generate enough money to repay the loan, they, out of their salary, supplement the mortgage difference.

By so doing, you have just introduced a new rule in your money game: the sponsoring rule.

What you are doing, in effect, is you are sponsoring someone to stay in your house.

If your mortgage repayment is 5 000.00, but your tenant is paying you 4 000.00 in rental, you are sponsoring your tenant by 1000.00. Your tenant is living a 5000.00 bucks lifestyle but it's costing them only 4000.00, courtesy of you.

You are saying to your tenant: please come and stay in my house and I will pay an additional 1000.00 every month to supplement your lifestyle.

This is indicated by arrow (8) on the field (Figure T). It shows your own income supporting your liabilities. There is no arrow 7 (profit) as was in figure S.

This should never happen to financially intelligent people.

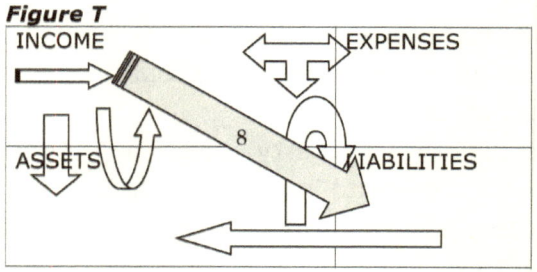

Figure T

This is what Robert Kiyosaki refers to when he asks the question: 'why would you knowingly lose money?' That is not financial intelligence. I am not saying that this is wrong or right.

All I am saying is, if that rental property was meant to be an investment, then you are having a negative return on your investments.

It is a pity that too many people do this and put forward other arguments to support this move.

The most common argument is: but the property is appreciating in value. While that may be true, or not, the fact is, you are currently still sponsoring someone to stay in your house. As far as cash flow is concerned, you are not winning the game.

The second rule of borrowing money intelligently is to ensure that not only does the loan repay itself, but you too must benefit from the loan immediately. Simply put, the loan must generate positive cash flow.

13. Does My Income Exceed My Expenses?

Using the rental property example, this means that the rental received must exceed the expenses incurred.

The expenses are not just the loan repayment:

- Interest and capital; but other expenses such as:
- Insurance – both property insurance and credit life insurance
- Maintenance,
- Taxes and levies,
- Management fees, as well as a
- Provision for vacancy factor. The vacancy factor means, if the property should become vacant, there must be money put aside from the rentals in previous months to cover the months when you have no tenant. If you don't make this provision, it takes one month without a tenant for you to fall behind on your mortgage repayments. If this situation persists for say three to six months, you are in danger of losing

your property to foreclosure or repossession.

This knowledge leads to financial intelligence.

Some might immediately say, properties that can produce those kinds of results are impossible to find.

Well, all the more reason to do your homework before you borrow money for such investments.

If you play your game with knowledge and understanding, you will find that there are plenty of opportunities out there.

But if you play your game without knowledge of the rules and the intelligence to apply them, then you will believe that success is impossible. This is the difference between borrowing for consumption and borrowing for growth or for performing assets.

SELF-ASSESSMENT

1. How do financially intelligent people borrow money?
2. What are the two important rules to consider before borrowing money?
3. What is the sponsoring rule?
4. Why is it important to pay off your first mortgage faster?

Chapter 12

12. POSITIVE CASH FLOW AND RE-INVESTMENT

"If your outgo exceeds your income, your upkeep is your downfall"
Unknown

> LEARNING OUTCOMES
> In this chapter you will learn:
> - Performing Assets
> - Re-investing principles
> - Self-sustenance
> - The difference between good money field and dysfunctional money field

There are other performing assets for which you can borrow money and have the positive cash rule above apply. If you borrowed money for a viable and profitable business, then you make sure the business produces enough money to repay its own liabilities and leave you with a profit. Many people seem to understand that if you borrow money for a business, then the business must repay its own liabilities and give you a profit.

But many more people do not apply the same rule when they get into real estate. It may be primarily because they don't see real estate as a business, but the truth is, they should.

It is not just a long-term investment, it is a business that needs to make money almost immediately. You don't borrow money for a business and allow it to make a loss while you are sitting around arguing that your business is growing in value. It is either giving you a profit now, or it's not worth going into. What's the point of keeping a job to finance a business?

14. The Re-Investment Rule

The next question is: what do you do when money comes back into your income quadrant from your performing assets? Your primary purpose in this game should be to grow, not to shrink. When money comes into your income quadrant, whether through your savings or from other investments, you send it right back to the Asset quadrant so that it can generate more cash.

This is the Re-investment rule and is represented by arrow (9) on the money field (Figure U).

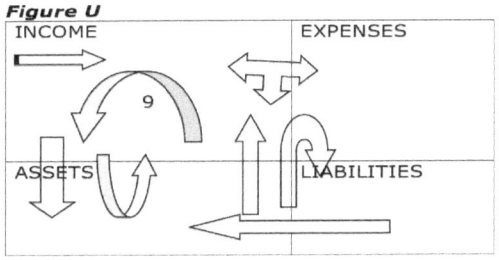

Figure U

This could arguably be the single most important rule on the money field that contributes to building wealth.

It is one thing to collect revenues; it is another thing to make profits, but it is quite another thing altogether to re-invest your profits.

At this stage some people might say, but that sounds miserly. I don't want to be stingy, I want to spend and enjoy my money now!

The answer is: if you want to enjoy your

money without worry, then this is exactly what you need to create. You need to create a system that can continually generate cash for you to enjoy. That starts with re-investing for growth.

For a lot of people, the only source of income is their job. They have nothing else to help them. I am not talking here about saving money forever and never getting to enjoy your money. I am talking here about creating a system that can help you generate more cash for your enjoyment.

15. The Self-Sustenance Rule

The self-sustenance rule is about building a system from which you can continue to live. When this system is set up, you will see how a financially intelligent person can start spending money. Not only from the meagre salary, but most or all of your expenses can start coming from your asset quadrant. Arrow (10) in Figure V shows that assets can support expenses.

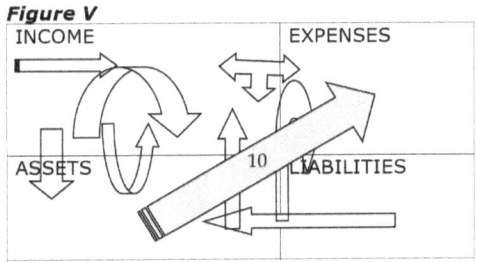
Figure V

This is what financial freedom is all about. It is about creating a system that can help you with your living expenses without you labouring hard for it.

Sure, it takes time to set up such a system, but it surely can be set up. Financial freedom is about systems. It is not the amount of money coming in, whether little or too much, it is a system that can keep it coming in whether you work it or not.

This is what is referred to as passive income. The river may start off as a trickle, and then it becomes a creek, and then a mighty river with lots of fish swimming your way. Now you have a system that can support you in all seasons.

Figure W
THE FINANCIAL GREEN LINE:

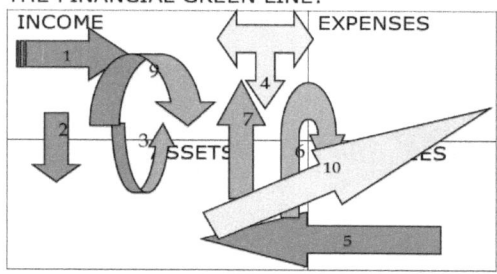

The above money field represents all the arrows on the field:
1. The Income Rule
2. The Pay Yourself First Rule
3. The Return on Investment Rule
4. The Balanced Split Rule
5. The Borrowing for Security and Performing Assets Rule
6. The Positive Cash Flow Rule
7. The Income from Liabilities Rule or The Profit Rule
8. (We skip The Sponsoring Rule since it is not a rule applied by the financially intelligent)
9. The Re-Investment Rule
10. The Self-Sustenance Rule

Now, compare this with the LIFE-STYLE focused diagram that we discussed in chapter five (replicated below) and choose.

Figure X

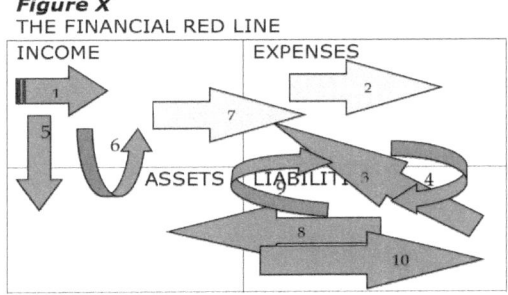

The Life-Style focused diagram is bleeding your resources. It is bleeding you to the ground. It is what we call the financial red line!

The Wealth-Style focused diagram is meant to help you grow. It is a breeding life, instead of a bleeding life. If you notice, Figure X, The Financial Red Line, shows that the play is mostly on the right side of the money field. The flow of money is focused on *expenses and liabilities*. This is the lifestyle focused diagram.

The diagram on the intelligent money field (Figure W) is focused on the left side of the money field, or on *income and assets*. This is the wealth-style focused diagram.

So, the question is are you focused on building a lifestyle or are you focused on building wealth?

The Re-investment Rule could arguably be the most important rule of wealth building

SELF-ASSESSMENT

1. What question do financial intelligent people consider before borrowing money, and which money rule requires them to ask this question?
2. What is the re-investment rule?
3. What is the difference between the life style focus and the wealth building cycle?

Chapter 13

13. FINANCIAL GOALS

"Becoming an expert at goal setting and goal achieving is something that you absolutely must do if you wish to fulfil your potential as a human being".
Brian Tracy

LEARNING OUTCOMES
In this chapter you will learn:
- Why people do not set goals
- Why it's important to write down goals
- How to successfully set goals
- SMART Goals

Success Through Goal Setting

Brian Tracy, quoted above, has written more

than 36 books and produced more than 300 audio and video learning programs, including the "Psychology of Achievement."

Let's look at some excerpts from some of his writings on Goal Setting. Goals enable you, among other things, to do the work you want to do, and to become the kind of person you want to be.

Yet, writes Tracy, according to the best research, less than 3% of people have written goals, and less than 1% review and rewrite their goals on a daily basis.

Why do so few people set goals? Here are a few basic reasons.

1. *They are simply not serious.* In other words, until you become completely serious and determined about your goals, nothing really happens.
2. *They don't understand the importance of goals.* As Zig Ziegler says: "Most people don't plan to fail, but there are many failures because people fail to plan." Until you have a goal, you have nothing to achieve. The plan hinges on the goal.
3. *They don't know how to do it.* Brian Tracy writes: "One of the greatest tragedies of our educational system is that you can receive 15 to 18 years of

education and never once receive a single hour of instruction on how to set goals."
4. *Fear. Fear of rejection. Fear of criticism. Fear of ostracism. Fear of failure.* People often hold back from setting worthwhile goals because every time they do set a goal, somebody steps up and tells them that they can't achieve it, or that they will lose their money or waste their time. *Fear of failure* is probably the greatest single obstacle to success in adult life. It can hold you back more than any other psychological problem. What would you do if you were not afraid?

If you can overcome obstacles and set well-defined goals, you can channel your efforts and focus your energy toward something important to you.

Goal setting gives you a target to aim at and enables you to develop the self-discipline to continue working toward your target rather than becoming distracted and going off in other directions.

When you look around you, will see that all achievement is the triumph of persistence.

You will see people everywhere who are struggling with, and overcoming adversities in order to accomplish something that is important to them. And so can you.

The Power of Writing Down Your Goals

Studies show that people who put their goals down on paper have a much higher level of achievement than those who don't.

If you want to be a high achiever, write down your goals – and read them repeatedly.

According to Tom Bay, in his book entitled *Look Within or Do Without*, Harvard Business School did a study on the financial status of its students 10 years after graduation. The Study found that:

- As many as 27% of them needed financial assistance.
- A whopping 60% of them were living paycheque to paycheque (that is, hand to mouth survival)
- A mere 10% of them were living comfortably.

- And only 3% of them were financially independent.

The study also looked at goal setting and found these interesting correlations:

- The 27% that needed financial assistance had absolutely no goal setting processes in their lives.
- The 60% that were living pay-cheque to pay-cheque had basic survival goals (such as managing to live pay-cheque to pay-cheque).
- The 10% that were living comfortably had general goals. They thought they knew where they were going to be in the next five years.
- The 3% that were financially independent had written out their goals and the steps required to reach those goals.

Well, what do you do with statistics such as these? Do you say, well, they seem too perfectly correlated perhaps just to make a point, or do you consider that there is merit in these findings?

While many of us have the degree, we did not get the education, and it does not matter what school you went to.

The real school is in the "University of Hard-knocks", called real life. Why would writing down goals make the difference? Why can't I just think generally about them?

Number one, writing creates a focus. When you actually have to come up with descriptive words to represent the picture you have in your mind, more questions about how you will achieve that will surface and you will have to answer them, and that provides you with clarity.

Secondly, once you get clarity, it may take you away from fantasyland and bring you down to the practicality of your desires. If you say I want to have a million bucks within a year, writing that down may bring you to ask, how much do I have to make per month, per week, per day? That will paint a different picture because now you have to face what is possible.

Smart Goals

Keep your goals SMART. This is an acronym that will help you in setting your goals.

S = Specific – not general like I want to be

rich, but how much do you want to be worth? You have to get specific in all areas of your finances.

How much of your debt do you want to have paid by when? How much savings do you want to accumulate by when? How much sales do you want to achieve by when?

M = Measurable – can you break them down? What is the unit of measure? What currency? How many units of sales per period?

A = Achievable – can other people of equal ability and skill, given the same opportunity, achieve them.

Achievability helps you to keep your head out of the clouds and out of fantasyland.
- Are there specific actions that can be taken to achieve this goal?
- Are you capable of doing this?
- Do you have the skills to achieve this?

List the skills or the tools it will take to achieve this.

R = Realistic – not pie in the sky; Can you match the specific skills that you have with this goal. (Not dependent on factors over which you have no control)

If you say I want to be a bestselling author; the first question is, can you write? The second question is, can you sell? The third question is, can you write a sellable book? The next question is, are you willing to do both – that is, write a sellable book and get out and sell it? Another question would be, are there readily available systems that you can follow to do this? As you can see, "realism", is brought about by a series of connected questions that need to be answered. Nothing should be left to chance.

T = Timely – set a timeline. Making a million within a year implies that each month you will have average revenue of not less than 83 333.33; which breaks down to a further 20 833.33 per week on average, which breaks down to a further average of 4 166.67 per day.

Now you can go back and ask yourself the preceding questions such as, is this realistic and achievable? Should I reduce the goal to half a million or should I increase the time to two years?

For each goal that you have, see if it can fit the mould as set out in the next page.

	GOALS AND DETAILS
SPECIFIC	
MEASURABLE	
ACHIEVABLE	
REALISTIC	
TIMELY	

Set your goals for each quadrant of the money field.

INCOME GOALS	EXPENSES GOALS
ASSET GOALS	LIABILITIES GOALS

SELF-ASSESSMENT

1. Why is it important to set goals?
2. How can you effectively set goals?
3. What are SMART goals?

The Money Field

Book 2

BOOK 2 - LIVING IN THE GAP

The Money Field book series – 3-in-1

Living in the Gap

Practical Strategies

Nelson Letshwene

"Never depend on single income. Make investment to create a second source"

Warren Buffett

Nelson Letshwene

INTRODUCTION TO BOOK 2

The Money Field digital version is a three-book series that started with *The Game of Money*, has progressed to this *Practical Strategies for Living in the Gap*, and will close with *Debt Management Principles* in book three.

All these areas are put together in one book in the print version as part one, part two and part three.

While it would be helpful to read book one in the series, the topics in this book are standalone topics and you will still learn a lot just by reading this book. You will not necessarily be disadvantaged if you have not read the first book in the series.

Some of the material in this book was formerly published in the book *Functional Mastery Over My Finances* (Reach publishers, 2008). Although some of the chapters that formed that book are in this book, they have been revamped, improved, updated, edited and made better for the sake of this new book series; and many other chapters of that book have been excluded.

I hope this book series will add value to the life of the reader, and help to increase financial literacy and other money skills that are so important in our lives today.

If you find this book helpful, feel free to give us some feedback or leave us a review for further improvements.

Thank you,

Nelson Letshwene
October, 2017
Gaborone, Botswana

PREFACE

THE MONEY MANAGEMENT MODEL

"Honesty is a very expensive gift. Do not expect it from cheap people."
Warren Buffet

In book one of this series, you would have experienced the money management model we call The Money Field.
This money management model that facilitates the money game, is a four-quadrant system that tracks your money from the time that it enters the income quadrant, and follows it all around The Money Field. It tracks money from the income quadrant to the various areas and categories of the expenses quadrant. It further tracks how money may leave "other

people's pockets", to come into your pockets and form obligations called your liabilities quadrant.

From your income quadrant, your main focus is to grow your asset quadrant. Financial success is often measured by the size of your asset quadrant, continually fed and supported by your income quadrant.

The two quadrants that take money away from you are the expenses quadrant and the liabilities quadrant, which reduces your net worth.

In this second book of the series, we focus on "practical strategies for living in the gap". "The Gap" is the distance between your current state and your desired state. In the game of money, you are always in transition from one state to another. You may be transitioning from low income to high income through strategies of multiple streams of income. This book has chapters that focus on those strategies.

You also need strategies of protection and sustenance. You will also encounter practical money management tools such as budgeting, and principles of increase like savings and investments.

In Practical Strategies for Living in the Gap, you will experience the real work that goes with money management. You will be challenged to employ the tools that are important in the physical management of your money. You are encouraged to either draw the tools in your private workbooks, or download a spread sheet that will get you involved in the real game of managing and taking control of your finances.

Thank you.

Chapter 1
1. LIVING IN THE GAP

"We devour the bread of charity because we are hungry; it revives, then slays us."

Kahlil Gibran

> **LEARNING OUTCOMES**
>
> In this chapter you will learn:
> - The implications of living in the gap
> - Tools for living in the gap
> - The psychology of reaching goals

A GAP is the distance between your current state and the state you will be in when your goal is achieved.

The setting of any goal creates a gap between where you are and where you intend to be. Managing this gap is what will determine whether you reach your goals or not. People fail to reach their goals only because they don't perceive the gap between where they are and where they want to go.

If you can know exactly where you are beginning, and perceive the distance where you are going, you have to get ready to live in the gap. It is vitally important to practically define the implications of your goals on your current life. You will have to change something and maintain the change until you reach your goals. When you say you want to lose weight because you like the new fashion that's out there, it does not mean if you went and bought small size clothes tomorrow you will be slim. There is a gap between where you are and where you want to go. Can you live in this gap?

What are the implications of living in this gap?

Once a goal is set, it will not achieve itself. A financial goal often implies a change in current lifestyle until the goal is reached.

If you are not someone who is accustomed to saving money, and now you decide that saving is going to be one of your goals, you must understand that the money that you want to start saving, will have to come from somewhere, which implies that some other area of your life will have to change. You have to choose what that area is, make adjustments, and commit.

You are either going to cut on something to save the money, or you are going to start doing something to generate the extra cash that you want to save. If you don't want to go out and make extra money, then you must learn about budgeting, and choose to cut something out.

The trouble with many people is that they want to have their cake and eat it. If you have identified your eating out money as the portion of your money that you would now like to put into savings, you must understand that now you have to cut down on eating out. This is where strict adherence to a tool called a budget may become useful.

If your goal is to get out of debt, you must understand that continuing to live on the credit card or on revolving credit is not going to work. You have to stop borrowing completely, and perhaps realise that your gap includes making more money to cover the existing debt.

A budget is a tool that will help you to live in

the gap. A debt management program is a tool you could employ to live in the gap. A weight management program is a tool that has to be your companion as you live in your gap.

If your goal is to be rich, then your gap will involve a wealth growing tool that you are applying as you live in your gap. But it has to be a wealth generating tool. The gap is not just a practical place, but it is also a psychological place. It speaks well of your commitment to your ideals. If you are committed to your WHY, your HOW will come easy.

The Psychology of reaching goals

Most goals, if not well calculated and thought out, can be daunting and therefore discouraging. You need to break your goals down into manageable chunks. It is important to know exactly where you are, exactly where you are going, and manage the gap in between.

SELF-ASSESSMENT

1. What does it mean to live in the gap?
2. What tools do you need to be able to live successfully in the gap?
3. What, according to you, is the best way to implement your "gap-strategy"?
4. What are some of the psychological issues associated with living in the gap?

Chapter 2

2. BUDGETING PRINCIPLES

The habit of saving is itself an education; it fosters every virtue, teaches self-denial, cultivates the sense of order, trains to forethought, and so broadens the mind.

T.T. Munger

LEARNING OUTCOMES
- What is a budget
- Budgeting principles
- How to create a budgeting worksheet

The Budget Spending Sheet

The trouble with so many people, is that they've never taken the time to understand what proper financial planning is all about. They always assumed they know, until they are in trouble. At the end of every month, there's that little sheet that comes out called a budget.

The biggest trouble is not that they don't want to plan, but the truth is they don't know what a budget is.

- They think by writing out an expense sheet every month that they are 'budgeting'. Can you imagine if the government did that? Do you see the minister of finance looking at how much VAT was collected this month, and then, and only then deciding what will be paid this month? (Would your salary be covered if you worked for government – you would wonder!) It's ridiculous. Yet, that's what many of us do every month.
- This "monthly budgeting" leads to increased frustration because it doesn't work.
    - That's why most of us toss it out the window and go to the loan sharks to borrow survival money.
    - That's why our credit cards are maxed to the limit.
    - That's why that squeaky bed and ragged sofa have not been

replaced yet ... it's because they never made it on the real budget three years ago ...because there was no budget ...no foresight!

A budget must be done _ONCE_ a year, and it must include two to five-year planning in it. What you do every month, is monitoring, not 'budgeting'. A budget gives you a chance to decide how much money you *want* to make, and what you *want* to save and spend for that year. It is not necessarily based on what you already have, but it gives you a chance to grow.

Most people have been living day to day for a long time. If they don't change this day-to-day living mentality, this will go on until retirement. They have set themselves up to fail ...

You might say, but I only have one job and it only pays me so much. Well, if what they pay you is enough to meet your long-term budget, good. If not, have you heard of the saying: 'think outside the box'?

To think outside the box, you must first determine what has been boxing you in. What limitations have you subscribed to? So, what should you do?

Your Annual Budget Principles:

First, make a list of everything you would like to achieve this financial year. A financial year may be the same as a calendar year, or it may start as a twelve months cycle from wherever you are. Some people choose their birth month as the first month of their planning year.

Draw a full year calendar and put it in front of you. You may have Quarterly totals for each quarter (Q1 – Q4)

JANUARY	FEBRUARY	MARCH	Q1
APRIL	MAY	JUNE	Q2
JULY	AUGUST	SEPTEMBER	Q3
OCTOBER	NOVEMBER	DECEMBER	Q4

Notice that each month of the year is financially unlike any other month. Notice the things that will happen only in those specific months and how those will affect your finances.

For example, Valentine's day will only happen in February; Easter will happen in April; Christmas will happen only in December. If you have school-going children, note the months in which you have to pay school fees. Notice months of family birthdays or family events. Notice your national calendar and see how national holidays affect your budget.

Now include all the fixed expenses that will happen every month of the year without variation. For example, your mortgage repayments or your rental is a constant figure all year round.

Now include your variable expenses on your budget. Be aware of seasonal differences. For example, your electricity bill will differ between summer and winter.

Take your time and include in your annual budget everything that you believe will happen this year, and what you would like to happen.

Add up all the costs for the year and see your total for the year. Now add up your projected income for the year. What is the difference between the projected expenses and the projected income? Do you have a deficit or a surplus budget?

If it's a deficit, what can you do now, before the year begins, to bridge the gap. What income producing projects can you initiate early on in the year?

If it's a surplus, what other investments can you think about?

Commitment

Tuberculosis (TB) is a curable disease, but the regiment is a long-term process. You have to take the medication for at least six months in most cases. You can't stop when you feel better after three months. If you don't take your medicine to the bitter end, you do get the bitter end, so to speak.

What is the point of going to the doctor if you are not going to take the prescription medicine? Many of us approach our finances like an ill-disciplined TB patient. We stop when we feel better!

You must commit and reap the benefits of a changed financial future, or, if you don't commit, you go on with your life and never know the difference.

Why is it that most people don't keep a

budget? There are various reasons: 'I don't make enough money to be on a budget', or 'Budgets are too restrictive', or 'I'm not good with numbers', or 'I am too ashamed because it exposes my ill-discipline with money.'

Well, for whatever reason you may not keep a budget, you are missing out on the possibilities of Financial Intelligence that you could develop as a result of understanding your finances.

As I have said before and will probably say it again: what you don't know about money will hurt you. So as far as money is concerned, ignorance is not bliss. The belief that a person does not have enough money to be on a budget indicates that the person does not understand the concept of budgeting.

Anyone with any amount of income, even a student, can create a simple budget that works, even as simple as the envelope method.

People on low incomes are probably in the greatest need of a budget to allow themselves to initiate new income producing projects early on in the year to improve their incomes.

Be aware that perhaps the most common

budget error is simple discouragement. Remember, if your budget doesn't work the first month you try it, don't become discouraged. Developing a realistic budget takes time. Habits change slowly, especially spending habits.

It may take three to six months or more before your budget begins to work well, (especially if you have a lot of debt to deal with. See Debt Management section).

Principles

- Guard your money. Don't waste it. Every time you spend your money ask yourself: 'is this expense helping me to achieve my financial goals?' If the answer is 'yes', go ahead and spend, if the answer is 'no', think twice ... and empower yourself!
- A budget allows you to take control of your finances. A budget gives you the ability to plan ahead. You make conscious decisions about how to spend your money, instead of spending on impulse.
- Beware of the 'more-money-in, more-money-out' syndrome. This means you

spend more simply because you have more. This is particularly dangerous if the extra money is temporary income. Just because you've got a salary increment does not mean you need to alter your spending habits. You could just invest the money for the future.
- If you earn on commission or are self-employed and therefore face a fluctuating income, you are more at risk of this syndrome if you don't use a budget. So, take charge of your finances by determining your monthly averages quickly and prescribing a budget that will work for you.

Prioritize and Categorise

Well, how do you start? Prioritise! First things first. You need to identify your living expenses.

- o You need to pay Rent, (you can't live on someone else's money);
- o Utilities (gas, water, electricity, - otherwise you'll be caught in the dark, cold and thirsty)
- o Transportation (fuel, taxi/bus fare)

> If you have a car, include in this category your car insurance, and maintenance.
> o Food – watch this spot, you can save a lot by eating at home or carrying your lunch pack and avoiding junk food. Childcare if you have kids. Telephone bill(s).

Next, begin a simple form of budget by dividing your actual income among predetermined priorities.

Then create a register or schedule for each priority (account).

Next divide your earnings among your priority accounts and enter each amount as a deposit in that account. You may use an envelope to separate the cash, or to separate the receipts each time you swipe your card.

Keep adding the amounts on these receipts to make sure that you don't exceed your allocated amount per category.

Finally, when you take money from that account, enter the transaction as a withdrawal from that account.

Don't forget the big question: 'is this expense helping me to achieve my financial goals?'

Don't pass up this opportunity to focus your financial resources on what is really important to you. It's well worth the small-time investment.

Keep receipts. Balance your cheque book regularly. Account for the ATM withdrawals. Check your bank statement for debit orders and stop orders to make sure they have gone through, so that you don't get that surprise call demanding payment.

Take control of your money through the power of a budget! Budgeting gives you the power to control your financial future. With a budget you are able to set goals and go after them.

For most people, the future is not what it used to be. But with a budget and proper planning, the future can start looking bright again.

If you fail to plan, you have planned to fail! Having said all that, it is actually a whole lot easier to go make extra money than to try to live a restricted life.

We human beings are freedom seeking beings not prison seeking. We want to grow, not shrink.

When you think about your income, you might realise that most of it comes from a sale of only one skill that you have.

The truth is, you have a whole lot of other skills that you are currently not selling. In the chapter on *Your Personal Money Tree*, we will talk about how to identify more of your skills and how to sell more of them for your expanded self.

Your budget on the Money field:

Income budget	**Expenses Budget**
o How much money would you like to make? o What is your plan	o Set category limits o Set total expense limits
Asset Budget	**Liabilities Budget**
o Your security assets o Your investment assets	o What is the monthly limit from your salary that should go to service debt? o Which categories of debt are you working with?

SELF-ASSESSMENT

1. State some budgeting principles
2. Highlight the difference between a budget and a spending sheet?
3. What is the importance of an annual budget?

Nelson Letshwene

Chapter 3

3. PRINCIPLES OF SAVING

"Growth investors will only play in opportunities that have consistent, above average returns ...Income investors are looking for immediate cash out in the form of rental, lease, interest, or dividends payment ..."
Loral Langemeier

LEARNING OUTCOMES
In this chapter you will learn:
1. The principles of saving
2. The Pay Yourself First principle
3. Your money's friends and foes
4. How to fund your emergencies

After we discoursed on budgeting principles, the next big question may be Savings Principles. We've already discoursed on reasons why it is difficult to save in chapter 9. Now we should look to make it work. This may not be as easy as it may sound.

To build a strong house, you need a strong foundation. If you build on sand, the wind and the storms will beat against your house and it may fall with a big crash. Building a strong financial house needs you to understand the fundamentals first. Getting out of consumer debt and simultaneously paying yourself first must be your priority.

Pay yourself first

Starting the habit of paying yourself first is important, not so much for the amount of money you can actually save, but for the psychological advantage of developing a very important habit. Trying to save while you are in uncontrolled debt may of course seem counterproductive.

Of course, debt costs you more than what your money will make in a savings account. Banks and other lenders collect a lot of interest from you, even up to 30% depending on the product you are using as well as your credit rating, while they only give you between 1% and 7%, for deposits you make with them, also depending on the package and the amount of your deposit. Of course, these vary from economy to economy.

While I strongly recommend that you consult with a trusted financial advisor on your personal financial matters, my simple advice would be to understand the kind of debt that you are carrying, and then figure out a way to increase your means so that you can get out of consumer debt. Getting out of debt is, in my books, not necessarily a priority, but making more money is definitely a priority, while you keep your intentions to whittle down consumer debt.

There is no point getting out of debt when you don't know how to make more money, because as soon as you are out, you will be right back in again. You have seen this happen before. I know it's not news to you.

There are of course different categories of debt and some of these are mentioned in the section on Debt.

Your Money's Friends and Foes

The next thing you need to understand about savings, are things that eat up your money, and things that make your money grow. "Where did all the money go?" is the question that many of us ask ourselves every month just after payday. We ask this because we don't know what's eating our money up. It's as if we've put it in pockets with holes in them. You need to understand your budget as was discussed earlier.

- Bad spending habits and indiscipline may be what you need to tackle and overcome.
- Another creator of holes in your pocket is of course those high interest rates. They are the termites that gnaw at your wealth bit by bit, like my lawn that was once so promising, but has now been reduced to a dusty patch of ground.
- For those of you who are prudent stewards of your money, you need to understand how inflation nibbles at your loot over time, and outsmart it by adding inflation adjusters to your

savings.
- Impatience, whose opposite will be discussed below, is another crippling factor in the construction of your financial empire.

Your Money's Friends

Two things, among others, that make your money grow, are compound interest and time! You can't build a house overnight. Not a strong house anyway!

An old truism about investing is this:
- Financial wealth is created over long periods of time, not day trading. If you get all your ducks in a row quickly, there is nothing that can stop you from becoming wealthy within a reasonable amount of time depending on what you do and your level of commitment.
- The second friendly element to the construction of your wealth is of course, Compound interest. Albert Einstein called compound interest the 8th wonder of the world.

Compound interest thrives on time. This is when your interest earns interest. With long term investment and compound interest, the sooner you start the better.

That old adage rings true: procrastination is the thief of, not only time, but also wealth in this case. Hopefully by now you are ready to ask the all-important question of "how much should I save"? Well, would you like to become a millionaire?

> If you invest 67.00 bucks per month starting at age 20, invest this at 11%, and at age 65 you will have a million bucks in the bank! That's only 2.25 bucks per day! It sounds extraordinary, but it's true! You do the maths!
>
> A 25-year-old will have to invest 117.00 bucks while a 30-year-old will have to part with 203.00 bucks to make the big bucks. The longer you wait, the more you will have to fork out. At 35, you need 357.00 bucks, while at 40 you will have to give up 635.00 bucks per month.

Time, Discipline and Compound interest should be your loyal friends in the construction of your future nest egg.

The above, of course, is the traditional way of making a million bucks. There are newer ways of making money and building wealth.

Well, if it seems so easy why don't we have more millionaires? Because young people don't think about savings until it's too late.

Older folks forget about inflation, which will play havoc with your money if you have no inflation adjusters in your savings.

Before you rush out to the bank let me state that there are different savings criteria that you need to follow:

Funding Your Emergencies

You need to distinguish between Pure Emergency Fund (PEF) and Non-Emergency Fund (NEF). *Non-Emergency Fund* (NEF) is the amount after all expenses have been paid and emergency allotment has been satisfied. It is also called the reserve fund.

Pure Emergency Fund, on the other hand, is the amount set aside for emergencies such as losing your job, car problems, or a non-reimbursable medical event.

Most experts recommend at least three to six months of expenses to be set aside for the "PEF" account. This should be done before any investing of "NEF" is done.

This money may be put in a very safe investment such as a call account, money market account, a fixed deposit or a 32-day notice account.

Since it is allocated as an emergency fund,

you don't want to lock it away into long term savings, but you also want to be able to have it earning reasonable interest. 32 days is fairly liquid.

If the emergency is very immediate, you could finance it with your credit card and then apply to your bank to release these funds to cover your credit card.

Many credit cards have a window in which you do not pay interest. Once this Emergency amount has been satisfied, then you should feel comfortable starting your investment program.

The last thing you want to do is have to liquidate your long-term investment portfolio to meet short-term obligations that were unexpected. Avoid cancelling a long-term insurance policy to meet a short-term emergency. We call this dipping into principal to meet income needs.

This is a pretty simple concept but an important one, as we need to be good shepherds of our financial resources and not find ourselves stressed out because of some unexpected expense. Plan, not fear, for the unexpected and stay calm and at peace with whatever happens. No matter how diligently you build your financial empire, failure to purchase adequate insurance can put you in a desperate hole in a heartbeat!

SELF-ASSESSMENT

1. What is the importance of starting a pay yourself first habit?
2. List some of your money's enemies and state why they are enemies.
3. List your money's friends and state why they are considered your money's friends.

CHAPTER 4

4. YOUR PERSONAL MONEY TREE

"You can only become truly accomplished at something you love… pursue the things you love doing, and then do them so well that people can't take their eyes off you."

Maya Angelou

LEARNING OUTCOMES

In this chapter you will learn:
1. How to find your own money trees
2. Personal skills inventory process
3. The importance of additional sources of income

"Money does not grow on trees" is a reality for a lot of people. But what does that mean? For the most part it means that making money is not easy. It means money is not a commodity that you could just pick off trees like you can pick summer fruit.

But what if we believed that money grows on trees? A belief that money grows on trees is equivalent to the belief that making money is easy.

In this chapter I want to talk about the money tree. I would like for you to suspend your belief that money does not grow on trees. I would like for you to consider the possibility that it does actually grow on trees. If it did, I guess your first question would be: where are the trees upon which money grows? What if I told you that you are the tree? The seeds are resident within you and the purpose of this chapter is to reveal to you your own "acres of diamonds" as Russell Conwell used to say.

Russell Conwell was a man who, in the 1930s went all over the United States telling people that they were standing on their own "acres of diamonds" if they only looked within. He tells of men who sold their lands and went to faraway lands to look for diamonds, only for diamonds to be discovered from the lands they sold. He tells of men who stopped three feet from gold and sold their equipment, only for the buyer of the equipment to mine the wealth. That speech is still available today and you can find it on the Templeton university website.

The Money Tree is the thing that can bring the cash in. All you have to do is nurture it and take care of it. We all have our own money tree(s).

How Do You Find Your Own Money Tree?

Think about yourself this way: if you have a job, you are probably selling a certain number of hours (usually eight) per day to an employer who is interested in a particular skill that you have.

The next question you have to ask yourself is: is that the only skill that you have? The answer is, for the most part: of course not!

But if you are like most people, the skill that your employer is buying from you is the only skill that you are selling, and therefore it is the only skill that brings money into your personal money field.

Many of us feel like we don't even own that

skill anymore because we have probably signed a non-compete clause with the employer "to never use that skill outside of the business of the employer". If that is the case, you may feel like the employer owns the money tree, the only money tree you have ever nurtured and developed.

Where then do I find another money tree? Before we think about other skills totally unrelated to your primary skill, consider your primary skill and figure out what other subsidiary skills you have learned that may or may not be related to the main skill itself. If you are an accountant for example, consider the fact that organisational skill, which your employer is not necessarily paying for, could be employed by you in other ventures. If you are a good lawyer, the chances are your public speaking skills are good, and if you found another topic over which you are passionate, you could make money being a motivational speaker or a trainer.

To have a good start in nurturing your money tree, it is important that you start with what you know. If you want to start a business, start it in the field that you already know.

Why do businesses fail, especially start-up

businesses? Loral Langemeier, author of *The Millionaire Maker* says most entrepreneurs fail because they choose to pursue entrepreneurship with new skills instead of with known skills.

People have a "dream" business in a field that they know nothing about, and instead of making money the day they open, they spend more time trying to figure out how that particular industry works. They can't be in the conversation because they don't know the language of that industry. So, they end up losing money instead of making money.

That would be like a teacher wanting to go into the hospitality industry like tourism, but because she has never operated there, she would have to spend much more time trying to learn the language of the industry instead of making money.

What do you think would be the fastest way to cash for a teacher? Should she not stay in the teaching industry? The reason she wants to get out may be because she feels she has not been making money in that industry. All she has to do now is change her revenue model. She has been receiving her money as an employee, now she can receive her money as an entrepreneur, perhaps by starting a private tutoring company; the key word being company.

That means she does not have to be the one teaching the lessons, but she has to manage the business. How? She still has her full-time job. There's only few weekends in a month. How is she going to run a tutoring business?

Here is a better question: how many students from the university or those waiting to go to tertiary institutions can you find that would like to make extra money on the weekend?

Of course, there are plenty. So, you hire them to give lessons to junior school kids? Yes. All they need is an entrepreneur who can manage them. Someone to do the marketing and get new students enrolled; a place to operate from; someone to manage the accounting and the scheduling. That's where the experienced teacher comes in. She selects those tutors who were best in their particular subjects and hires them; then get junior school kids to sign up. That is a teacher's fastest way to cash. She could be making money within two weeks.

A musician could start a coaching team for kids wanting to start a band. A sports teacher could teach tennis lessons, etc.

You get the idea. Focus on what you know

now, before breaking into a field you don't know. The keyword in business is cash flow. Figuring out the fastest way to cash could generate money for your future "dream" business.

Personal Skills Inventory

Draw up a personal skills inventory list. As we mentioned earlier, always start with what you know. Look at your current job and figure out how many skills it takes to accomplish it.

By that I don't mean how many people, I mean, how many skills, all of which are performed by you, does it take to get your job done.

What exactly do you do at your job? List all the activities regardless of what your official job description says. Don't just write Human Resources. Break it down.

- o Do you do recruitment and hiring?
- o Do you headhunt?
- o Do you interview?
- o Do you train?
- o Do you develop training material?

- o Do you deal with Industrial relations issues?
- o Do you counsel employees?
- o Do you liaise with industry partners in any way?
- o Do you deal with payroll?
- o Do you do exit interviews?
- o Do you deal with CVs?

All these are different skills that it takes to do your job, and if you think about it, you could specialise in any one of these and become an expert in that field. Can you see that?

Take about 90 minutes of uninterrupted time and list your entire skill set. Think about everything. What did you do when you were younger? What are some skills that you applied in previous jobs that you no longer use now? Is there a way you could build businesses around these skills?

In the next chapter, we look at how you can sell these skills and bring more money into your money field.

INCOME	EXPENSES
Tools for bringing more income ○ Skills ○ Talents ○ Education/qualifications ○ Business	
ASSETS	LIABILITIES

SELF-ASSESSMENT

1. "Money grows on trees" – explain
2. What is the process of finding your own money trees?
3. How can you break down your current skill into multiple skills?
4. Which skills remain "unemployed" in your own personal life?
5. What will you do about your own unemployed skills?

Chapter 5

5. MARKETING YOUR PERSONAL SKILLS

"It's not how much money you make, but how much money you keep, how hard it works for you, and how many generations you keep it for."

Robert Kiyosaki

LEARNING OUTCOMES

In this chapter you will learn:

1. Various entities that will be interested in your skills

2. Entities with vested interest in your particular skill set

Who Has Money to Give You?

The question of who has money to give you has several layers: First, who would be interested in your particular skill set and talents, as well as the products and services that you would offer?

Second, if they are interested, do they have money to acquire your services?

Third, do they have the authority to make a purchase decision?

Identifying your particular target market using these layers helps you not to waste time with people that are just interested but can't buy either because they have no money or no authority. Market research is simply you trying to figure out who will pay you for what you can do.

There are various categories of entities with money, and each one of them uses a different method to acquire services. Consider the following list of entities with money:

1. **Individual consumers**

    If your product, service, skill, or talent is geared towards individual consumers, you need to start separating those who interest, money, and authority from the rest. Understand the buying behaviour of individual consumers.

2. Businesses

Businesses generally only buy goods and services that will help them to either be more profitable or more efficient in carrying out their core business. Is there a way that you can align your skills, talents, goods, or services to fit in with the objectives of the businesses you are trying to sell to?

3. Government

Governments acquire goods and services through the tendering system. If you want to sell to government, you need to familiarize yourself with the tendering system.

Many governments are outsourcing a lot of services that do not form the core of their functions. If you can align your skills and talents with some of these you could benefit.

Another thing which is peculiar to government is that they have a lot of programs that people out there do not understand or know how to access. If you understand these services you can make it your business to help others understand and access these programs for a fee. There are always opportunities that are worth exploring.

4. Non-government organisations (NGO's)

To be able to utilize your skills and talents with NGO's you have to align yourself with what they do and understand their objectives.

Each one of these entities use a different method and motives to acquire services. Depending on the area in which you would like to focus, it is important to learn what that field requires. Generally, businesses and government have the most money, and figuring out how to sell to them might be your fastest path to cash.

The only way to make lots of money from individual consumers is you must sell to a lot of them; whereas you could make one transaction to a business or a government agency and make more money than selling to individual consumers. Businesses and governments, however, take a lot of time to make decisions, so you need to be patient.

Who Has Vested Interest?

Another way to attract money is to look at your skills and consider who would succeed if you succeeded. In other words, who has vested interest in your success.

If you are a baker, then the flower companies would benefit if you succeed because you would be utilising their flower. You could therefore go and ask them to support your project. They could fund you or support you with resources or space.

Depending on your set of skills, you could go into joint ventures with other people. You should build or join what Napoleon Hill, author of *Think and Grow Rich* called The Mastermind Group.

Do not think that you can be successful on your own. Work with others. Leverage your skills. Get support. Give support to others. There are many ways to make money. Money does grow on trees if only you would plant the seeds, nurture yourself and align yourself with the right resources.

You can get into network marketing systems. You can invest on the stock market. You can make money on the Internet. You can build your own business. You can support other people's businesses through your own business. Life is a collaborative effort. Life is a joint venture. And money grows on trees!

You could approach big business that would have vested interest in your success to incubate your business. They can house you, or give you technical support.

SELF-ASSESSMENT

1. What are your own personal skills
2. How do you identify them?
3. Who are the entities with the most money?
4. How do you know who might have vested interest in your success?

Chapter 6

6. HOME, SWEET HOME!

"No man's family can fully enjoy life unless they do have a plot of ground wherein children can play in the clean earth ..."

George Clason

> LEARNING OUTCOME
> In this Chapter you will learn:
> - What to consider when buying or building your Home
> - The buyer's checklist

We all have dreams of prosperity. We would like to live in a dream house in a plush neighbourhood, driving our dream car and having our dream family, and live happily ever after! Does the saying, "Rome was not built in a day" ring a bell? How loud is the bell, you ask?

If you go and ask most of the people that are currently living in their "dream" house, driving their dream car, they will tell you their previous addresses were in places they were not eager to have visitors in, and they will show you pictures of their first cars, or not, and you won't believe it.

Unless one is born into wealth or into royalty, or wins the lottery, or inherits some riches from some rich relative, most of us have to sweat it out to make it.

How do you buy or build your dream house? It's pretty much the same way that you get to your dream car. You start with a small affordable car that will get you from 'A' to 'Z'. After a few years of working, you don't just want to go from 'A' to 'Z', you want to get there 'in style'. Now you trade in your old car or sell it so that now you have a deposit for a car that will get you there in style. After a few more years, you don't just want to get there in style, you want to make a statement and also get there in comfort or Luxury. Now you sell your 'style' car so that you can get your luxury car.

How long between your 'A to Z' car and your luxury car? Not a few months! In most cases, it takes years.

Buying a home can follow a similar pattern. But many of us like short cuts, we want that posh address now, so we pay exorbitant rentals to keep up appearances, while the reality is that we are bleeding our finances to the ground. Let us consider a method you could use to acquire your dream house.

Start Early

This, however, is not for the impatient. In your younger years after you've been working for a few years and you want to acquire a home loan, you go to the bank and the bank wants 20% down as a deposit before they can lend you the money.

Banks normally calculate 30% of your monthly income as your repayment, and they work out how much they should lend you.

If you have other loans, some banks will deduct those payments out of this 30% and work out your loan amount based on what you can pay.

You find it very difficult to raise 20% of your

dream house.

In addition to this, you need to have money for transfer fees and all other initial costs.

The task seems impossible. So you get discouraged and do nothing other than complain about how impossible banks are. Big mistake! What you should do is, go back to the bank and find out how much they will lend you, and take whatever they are willing to let you borrow. If you have a subsidy scheme from your employer, this will definitely help. With that amount go and buy the house that you can afford. Granted, that's not your dream house, but, congratulations! You are a homeowner.

Before that step however, make sure you consult your estate agent. They will tell you a whole lot more about the intricacies of buying a home than I can in this short chapter.

They will tell you about transfer fees, lawyers' fees, bond fees, and maybe their fees. Don't despair; it's how it works.

Another big question is: To build or to buy? Building may not be as cheap as you've been made to believe. Check with your real estate agent.

The Buyer's Checklist

As is often said in real estate circles: Location, location, and location is the key!

When buying a home, your location is the most important element. This is a very important investment and you must guard it carefully, especially if you are going to sell it so that you can buy a better home.

Get your checklist out and examine your potential new home.

- Check for cracks in the walls, both inside and outside.
- Smell for damp and feel plastered walls for moisture.
- Be wary of new paint or wallpaper - this could be hiding cracks or damp.
- Check for woodworm and rot if the property has wooden window frames, doors and floors.
- Inspect bathrooms to see if they are well ventilated, and check if the taps work and the toilets flush properly. You wouldn't want a blocked toilet after you move in now would you?
- Any missing roof tiles? – Missing tiles could lead to leaking and other water damage.
- Check for large trees near the building as

their roots could damage the foundations.
- Check the garden to see if you will need to fell any trees.
- Are there boundary walls?
- If not, and you have pets, it might be advisable to erect them.
- If there are electric fences, gates and garage doors, check if they are in working order and whether they need a service.

Ask the seller as many questions as you possibly can.
- Find out why he is moving.
- Ask about crime in the area – or phone the local police station for crime statistics. Now, are you happy?

Next, pay that house off as quickly as you know how.

Depending on prevailing interest rates, by adding an additional two to five hundred bucks to your monthly bond, you will cut down not just interest, but the repayment period. In as quick as seven to ten years, your house could be paid off.

After you pay it off or you have taken a huge chunk of the bond off, you may now consider selling.

Since this is not your dream home yet, you can either turn it into your dream home through extensions, and improvement if there is room for that, or you can sell.

But I'm sure you've learnt a lot about homeownership. Now get ready for the big leagues.

Since property values tend to appreciate over time, even though not all the time, especially if it's in the right location, the value of that house in seven to ten years may be a considerable amount.

Now you can approach the bank and ask them to lend you money for your dream house!

You have more than enough money as deposit, and you can pay off the transaction costs! Now you are on your way to living happily ever after.

If that still does not give you your dream house, repeat the above process, or work on expanding your house to suit your style. If you start in your late twenties or early thirties, by the time you are in your fifties, you will be in your fully paid dream house.

If it is that simple, why don't more people own houses? Well, probably because of the short cut and the quick fix mentality that we are so accustomed to. What you don't know about money will hurt you!

Real Estate investing has a lot of issues that

you should understand. Commit yourself to learning and growth.

SELF-ASSESSMENT

1. What is the importance of starting early when you want to buy or build a home?
2. Why is it important to have a deposit when you borrow money for a home?
3. What are some things that are important on the buyer's checklist?

Chapter 7

7. INFORMATION – THE PAPER TRAIL

"You must gain control over your money or the lack of it will forever control you."

Dave Ramsey

> LEARNING OUTCOMES
> In this chapter you will learn:
> - Steps of Information Gathering
> - Classification of Information

The interesting thing about money is that, although largely invisible, it hardly goes anywhere without leaving a paper trail. In this chapter, we will follow the paper trail. The purpose of this chapter is to help you determine where you are in your money game.

Unless you know where you are, and you fully understand how money has been flowing on your money field, can't determining exactly where you want to go and how you are going to change the flow of your money to allow you to go there.

Many people are quick to set financial goals without knowing exactly where they are, but they wonder why they are not getting there. The job of determining your position on the money field may be tedious, but unless you do it, you might as well not continue with the course. Many of us just know that 'we're in trouble'. Or that money is going out faster than is coming in and we can't figure out why. We are living from emergency to emergency, and therefore, our lives are an emergency.

Gathering information and understanding that information will go a long way in helping you understand what is going on in your financial field.

There are FOUR basic things we will have to do in this chapter. If you are serious about taking control of your money, you cannot skip this step. Without this step there is no course. For some people the work might be less than what is suggested here because they've already been running some system.

But for those who have never started before, please be patient with yourself and allow yourself to do this very important step. Here are the FOUR basic steps you will have to follow, and we will explain each of them herein.
- Information Gathering
- Classification of Information
- Choosing an Accounting Period
- Physical Arrangement of Information

Please note that even if you intend to use a computer software program, you still have to take the above steps.

Information Gathering:

Let's start with available information and then we will move on to seek missing data.
Where is my money coming from and where is it going?
A: If you are employed, you probably have a *Pay Slip*.
What information can you find on your pay slip?
- Your gross earning
- Your income tax payment
- Your medical aid information

- Your pension fund contribution
- Any other deductions that come directly from your employer like loans, life insurance, etc.
- Your net take-home pay

While the purpose of your pay slip is to answer the question, where is my money coming from, you will also find on it information about where some of your money is going.

Your BANK STATEMENT is another source of information. What information can you find on your bank statement?

- Your income that gets paid by your employer directly into your bank account, i.e. your take home pay that remains after employer based deductions.
- Any other deposits that you make into your account – it would be a good idea to determine the source of these deposits by keeping your deposit slips. You will also find on the bank statement information about your direct debits or your bank stop orders.
- Another piece of information that you will certainly find on your statement is bank charges or interests earned or charged.

- If this account is a Cheque account, you can trace all payments through the cheques that have been written by doing a process of *bank reconciliation*.
- If this account has a debit card that you use to make purchases, then you will have to do some work to determine what the expenses charged were for. (This may be slightly difficult if you are a kind of person who does not keep receipts.) The name of the store and the amount of the purchases will appear on your statement and perhaps you can trace what it was you were buying from that store.
- If you use your card at an ATM (Automated Teller Machine) to withdraw money, then the trick is figuring out what you did with the cash that was withdrawn
- You may find here also information about returned deposits (or bounced cheques) debited back or charged back

OTHER INFORMATION TOOLS:

If information is neither on your pay advice slip or your bank statement, and you are a kind of person who uses a lot of cash, then your best bet to gather this other information is to keep receipts every time you spend money.

If the receipt does not say what you were buying, then it will help you to note on the receipt what it is you were buying.

This information will help you when you are classifying your transactions for analysis.

Classification of Information

The best way to work with information is to classify it in a way that is meaningful to you. You classify information by creating *categories*.

Categories help you to handle the amount of information you create in an organised manner.

Second, it will help you to make decisions on certain categories by tracking them.

You might, for example, notice that your "eating out" expenses could be controlled more, or your phone bill can be curbed, etc.

Below is a list of possible categories. You don't have to use them all, and you can create your own that are more meaningful to you. All you have to do is avoid over generalising, or being overly specific.

Rent/Mortgage

Utilities: - Water, Electricity, Gas
Groceries
Auto: Fuel, Service, Insurance
Telephone: - Cellular phone, Home Telephone Line, Other Line (e.g. Fax/Internet)
Clothing
Give-away-money (gifts, tithe, charity)
Emergency fund
Insurance
Savings
TV – satellite/licence
School fees/Childcare
Laundry
Personal care (hair, etc)
Entertainment
Hobbies (e.g. books, CD's)
Personal Development (Further education, special subjects, special books, etc)
Household Furniture/appliances
Household helper (Maid/ gardener/ babysitter/ personal assistant, etc)

SELF-ASSESSMENT
1. What is the paper-trail?
2. On which documents will you find your important information?
3. How should you go about gathering information?
4. Why is it important to classify information?

Chapter 8

8. PHYSICAL ARRANGEMENT OF INFORMATION

"Empty pockets never held anyone back. Only empty heads and empty hearts can do that."
Norman Vincent Peale

> LEARNING OUTCOMES
> - Choosing an accounting period
> - Physical Arrangement of Information
> - How to determine where your money's coming from and where it is going

The next thing you will have to do with your information is physically arrange it in such a way that you can easily access it. It does you no good even if you keep receipts of everything if at the end of your chosen *accounting period*, you can't find it or it takes you as long to find it.

You have to designate a physical place in your home where your financial data is stored. What is the purpose of keeping physical information? There are a number of reasons why you might want to keep this data:

- First and foremost, the presence of physical data helps you keep accurate records, instead of guessing what you think you paid. In case of a dispute that you paid something, you can produce a receipt
- Many people miss out on tax deductible expenses because they can't prove that they did pay simply because they lost the receipt

There are a number of tools you can utilise to physically store your data.

A filing Cabinet

An Arch-lever file

A filing box

A place in your home or office

Now that you have a designated place to store your information, it is not enough to just throw it in that drawer or cabinet. You need to create *physical categories.*

You have created classification categories, now you need to decide how your information will be arranged. It can be arranged in one of two ways:
- Per Accounting Period
- Per Category

Storing data by Accounting period means you file one month's information separately, and then you just arrange it by dates.

If you are using *accounting software*, you will just record your transactions as per the dates as they occur, and the software will sort them out by categories, and you will still be able to figure out how much you are spending on each category.

If you keep your information by *category*, it means of course that it does not matter whether this phone bill was for three months ago or for this month, they all go into the same place, but you will still have to arrange them by *dates* so that you can find them easily when you are looking for them.

If you use category filing, make sure that you do not create a category for each receipt, or you might run out of storage space. That is why creating your classification categories, is important.

You will also notice that some bills like

school fees, for example, don't appear every month if you pay your school fees per term instead of monthly, so you might have that space having only four receipts per year.

You therefore might want to lump smaller categories together for the sake of filing space.

A category like *utilities* could include all utilities like water, electricity, telephone, and gas.

If you use *period* classification, you will only need 12 files for the year, or just one Arch-Lever file for the year, instead of 15 or 20 little files depending on the number of categories you create.

So, whether you buy a large file box, or clear out a drawer in your bedroom, or install a new program on your computer, the same principle applies: You can only stay organized if there's a physical place for all the paper and information you need to track throughout the year. No matter the system, create your categories in advance. Then whenever you have an important piece of information to save, it will already have a home. These are some of the key file/folder categories for your project:

Expenses: This cabinet drawer/box/file

holds all your bills from utilities to medical bills to taxes.

You can further subcategorise your expenses folder so that you can track the telephone bills, utilities, groceries, petrol and travel, or rental, etc.

Your next category is Banking. This folder will help you keep monthly statements, cancelled cheques and deposit receipts. At the end of the month when you do your bank reconciliation, all the information will already be in one place.

Next is your Investments folder. Your insurance policies and any other investments documents go into this folder. This will also help you to monitor how you are doing as an investor.

Choosing an Accounting Period

This should be relatively easy to do. All you do in this step is decide whether you will file your information weekly, fortnightly, monthly, bimonthly or quarterly.

If you are a beginner, I will avoid a longer period and stick to an average period such as a MONTHLY period. In fact, in the beginning, to gain momentum, it might help you to file weekly, just until you pick up momentum and you are serious about this process.

Then you can move off to monthly and keep it there. Your accounting period can coincide with your bank statement period so that you can do your bank reconciliation easily.

Some bank statements start say on the 7th to the 6th and most people like working from the 1st to the 30th. Don't get thrown off if your statement is like that.

The bank normally starts on the day that you opened your account and will choose that as your statement period.

It is much easier to keep the same date or you could ask them to change your statement period to start at the start of the month to the end of the month. What is the importance of an accounting period?

An accounting period allows you to compare, say last month with the month before. An accounting period provides a yardstick against which you can measure your progress.

Information-Gathering Sheet

You may benefit from a use of an information-gathering sheet. As we said, you can use a weekly information sheet, or a monthly sheet. This is a sheet with days of the week on the left, and categories at the top, and each time you spend money in a particular category, you record it there. Here's an example.

	Transport	Food	Phone	Other
Monday				
Tuesday				
Wednesday				
Thursday				
Friday				
Saturday				
Sunday				

You may of course design your own sheet that suits your needs better. You may also have a monthly sheet with dates, 1 to 31 on the left, and categories at the top. The trick will be not to forget to record your financial activities, or to leave it until you forget what the receipt was for.

SELF-ASSESSMENT
1. What is an accounting period?
2. What tools can you use to physically store data?
3. What is the purpose of keeping physical information?
4. Which categories are relevant to you?
5. What is the use of having an information gathering sheet?

Chapter 9

9. CREATING RECORDS

"Wealth is the ability to fully experience life."

Henry David Thoreau

> LEARNING OUTCOMES:
>
> In this chapter you will learn:
> - Recording of Information
> - Income and Expense Statement
> - Cash flow Statement
> - Balance Statement

This chapter could be the most practical of all of them since it involves the recording of all the information that you have gathered in a significant manner. Taking this step is as important as the steps you have taken in the previous chapter. However, without this step, all you have done in the previous chapter will be in vain.

If you are utilising an accounting software, this will be easy since all you have to do now is enter the data according to the decision you have made.

After this, with most computer software packages, all you have to do is ask it questions and it will whip up for you in a matter of seconds the kinds of reports that you require. Some packages may even offer you some analysis to help you understand the figures.

You will do well to remember that these packages cannot make up your mind for you, so you still have to make decisions and interpret the information according to what your goals are. Now that you have your information at hand, we can start talking about creating your financial baseline.

Bank Reconciliation Statement

One of the processes that will help you to have correct information is the process of

Cheque Book Balancing or Bank Reconciliation Statement.

The purpose of reconciling your records with those of the bank as reflected on your bank statement, is to make sure that you and the bank are in agreement about the amount of money that you really have.

It is possible that you would think you have a certain amount of money in your bank account, meanwhile the bank has increased their bank charges, and you write a cheque that will bounce back to you. Or a cheque deposit that you have made has been bounced or returned to the drawer for one reason or another.

Or your bank statement is reflecting a balance bigger than what you thought you had, because a cheque that you wrote has not yet been presented to the bank for clearing.

Cheque Book Balancing

The process of bank reconciliation really starts with you balancing your own cheque book.

Depending which bank you are with, each cheque book has a Transaction form or a cheque stub upon which you should keep a record of each transaction that you make. This form allows you to record each withdrawal or deposit, keeping a 'running balance' at all times.

If you balance your cheque book every time you use your cheque book, you will almost always know approximately how much money you have in your bank account.

If you have a debit card attached to the account, you will have to remember to come and update your cheque book after each charge, so that you are always up to date with your account.

Now that you have kept your records straight, you can now compare your records with the records of the bank, to make sure that there is agreement.

This is the process of bank reconciliation. You basically compare your records with those of the bank, noting the differences and adjusting until you are in agreement.

Other Essential Financial Records

The purpose of creating Financial Records is to figure out where you are at in the financial game. To simplify this process, your records may contain basic lists, to begin with. You first list is of course a list of all your sources of income

Your next list is a list of all your usual expenses. Then comes the dreaded list of debts – all your debts. The next list is a list of all your assets. With these lists you will be creating three statements:

Section A: Income and Expense Statement

Your <u>Income and Expense Statement</u>, otherwise referred to as you Income Statement = serves to compare your income with your expenses.

Expenses do not only refer to cash expensed, but expenses include such things as your accounts like your telephone account, whether you paid it that month or not. When the bill arrives, it is an expense because you have already consumed (whatever it is the telephone company sells, i.e. talk time). Likewise, when your water bill arrives, whether you have paid it or not, it is an expense because you have already consumed the water.

Section B: Statement of Cash Flow

You <u>Statement of Cash Flow</u> will monitor the flow of your cash. This statement focuses only on hard cash. You don't include money someone else owes you if you have not yet received it, and you only record cash as it goes out. This is different to your income statement because some cash will go to other items that are not classified as 'expenses', such as savings, etc.

Section C: Balance Sheet

Then you will create your Balance Sheet. This represents your net-worth. This statement is not as fluid as the first two. It is sort of like a picture over a certain period of time, usually a year or more.

It is a list of all your assets up to that particular time, as well as all the liabilities pitied against such assets.

For example, while you might list your house as an asset, the mortgage on the house is the liability pitied against the asset. The difference between the value of the house and the amount of the mortgage still owed, represents the real value of the house to you.

That is, if you sold your house today at that value, you will have to settle the mortgage first, and what remains could be said to be your real asset.

From all these statements, you will be able to get your Net Worth.

What is your growth strategy going forward?

Income Strategy	Expense Strategy
Asset growth Strategy	Debt Strategy

SELF-ASSESSMENT
1. Give reasons why it is important to balance your statement or cheque book
2. List and highlight the differences by defining the three types of financial statements
3. What is a bank reconciliation statement and why is it important?
4. How does the cash flow statement differ from the income statement?

The Money Field

Book 3

BOOK 3 – The Trap Of Other People's Money

The Trap Of Other People's Money

"Neither a lender nor a borrower be"

Shakespeare

Nelson Letshwene

"Creditors have better memories than debtors"
Benjamin Franklin

****

"A man in debt is so far a slave"
Ralph Waldo Emerson

Nelson Letshwene

INTRODUCTION TO BOOK 3

This three-book series has covered The Money Game, Strategies for Living In the Gap, and now comes to "The Trap of Other People's Money", or Debt Management Systems.

While it would be beneficial to read the first two books in the series, the topic of this book is also a stand-alone topic and you can learn a whole lot by just understanding the subject of debt on its own merit.

The first book in The Money Field Series, The Money Game, covered the concept of the four quadrants of the money field upon which the game of money is played. This third book only focuses on the one quadrant that makes up the Liabilities quadrant.

To understand the other quadrants of The Money Field, it would be important to read the other two books in the series.

We focus on debt in this book only because it is the biggest trap that stops people from focusing on the number one goal of building wealth by growing their assets.

While the expenses quadrant is where lifestyle can be changed, the liabilities quadrant is a double-edged sword. In the hands of the financially illiterate, debt can be a dangerous tool to use. In the hands of the financially literate, it can be a helpful tool. It is important to understand this subject on its own merit.

In this third book, we have added another chapter, an Appendix, that focuses on practical questions and explanations about debt instruments. The Q & A on debt answers many questions regarding the structure of debt and what practical strategies one can apply to dealing with specific debt instruments.

I hope this book will add value to the life of the reader, and help to increase financial literacy and other money skills that are so important in our lives today.

If you find this book helpful, please feel free to give us some feedback or leave us a review.

Thank you,

Nelson Letshwene

Nelson Letshwene
October, 2017
Gaborone, Botswana
nelson@moedi.net

Nelson Letshwene

Chapter 1
1. WHY DO PEOPLE WANT TO LEND YOU THEIR MONEY?[7]

"Opportunity is missed by most people because it is dressed in overalls and looks like work."
Thomas Edison

Why is it that so much of the world is eager to get their money into your pocket?
The World Bank and the International Monetary Fund (IMF) are trying to get their money into the pockets of countries around

---

[7] This article was also placed on www.7moneyskills.wordpress.com by the author of this book.

the world. Banks are trying to get their money into the pockets of businesses around the globe.

Financial institutions that used to focus only on your protection like Insurance companies are now in the lending space, eager to get their money into your pockets. Mind you, this is the same money that you have contributed to them as your premiums for protection. Now they want you to borrow it.

Banks and other financial institutions have intensified their marketing efforts to get you to borrow their money. Micro lending organizations are popping up everywhere.

Even if you are already in debt, many companies are still eager to have you put *their* money into *your* pockets.

What is in your pocket that so many institutions would like to get their money there? What do they see in there that you do not see?

There are really two important things that the world of lenders would like to take from you: your earning potential and your assets.

If your earning potential can make other people rich over time, why would you not use it to your own advantage?

Graduates don't have assets other than their earning potential. Lenders load them up with loans so that over their life time, they can labour for these financial institutions.

Those who have assets have collateral, and lenders would like to get their claws on these hard-earned assets.

Countries with natural resources get loaded up with World Bank and IMF loans and end up losing not only their resources over time, these institutions even use the country's labour resources to get their money out. They claim they are creating jobs, but people work for them to get the country's resources out. These people end up poor at the end of their lives because even they are loaded up with personal debt.

In John Perkins[8]'s book, we learn of dirty secrets of how the world would like to own your resources.

If you are caught in this web of other people's money, it is important that you free yourself as early as you can.

This book teaches you the tools of debt or instruments used to bring other people's money into your pockets. It goes on to show

---

[8] Perkins, J. *Confessions of an Economic Hit Man*, Penguin, 2004

you the structure of debt, or what the trap is made up of so that you can disentangle yourself easily. It then discusses strategies for eliminating debt and staying out of debt, thus keeping your own money working for you, instead of it working for other people.

You have enough resources over your lifetime to make yourself wealthy. You do not need to be in a hurry to take other people's money. You need to be smart enough to employ your own money and resources to enrich your own life.

I hope this instalment of the third book in The Money Field Series will enlighten you and help you to take charge of your economic power.

SELF-ASSESSMENT

1. What is your experience with people wanting to lend you their money?

Chapter 2
2. OTHER PEOPLE'S MONEY

"Do not spit in the well – you may be thirsty by and by".
Russian Proverb

> LEARNING OUTCOMES
> In this chapter you will learn:
> - The necessity of Debt
> - The Debt planning system

Before we talk about other people's money, it may be helpful to talk about our own money. Our world is run on the principle of cause and effect. You reap what you sow. You cannot reap more than you have sowed. Our own money, more often than not, come to us as a result of the sale of our own skills, talents, capabilities, and energies in the market place to willing employers.

There is a saying that "there ain't no such thing as a free lunch".

Our money is a reward for trading in the market place. It seems therefore that life is a process of trading one thing for another.

Once we have traded our own energies and have acquired money, we in turn go and trade the money in the market place for goods and services, according to our needs, wants, and desires.

When we run out of money in the market place, we go back to sell more of our energies to acquire more money so that we can go back in the market place to acquire more goods and services.

As long as each one only trades as much money as they are able to make through their energies, the system seems to stay in balance.

The problem begins when I start wanting more goods and services now, than my hard-earned money can acquire right now. This is when I start employing, other people's money.

When I use other people's money today, money I have not yet earned, I am making a promise to them that I will devote a portion of my energies, skills, talents, capabilities, tomorrow, to earn their money for them.

Unfortunately, they inform me, that tomorrow, the prices of goods and services will be higher than today. So, if I use their money today, I must be willing to bring back tomorrow's money, which is higher than today's money.

Hoping that the price of my labour will be higher tomorrow, I agree and sign on the dotted line. I remain indebted to the money lender until I can pay him all of tomorrow's money. If the price of my labour does not go up as I had hoped, I start to fall behind.

Debt, is nothing but other people's money. Other people's money is other people's energies, skills, talents, and capabilities.

Unfortunately, or fortunately, depending on how you look at it, we have created on our planet, "legal persons" who do not have flesh and blood like natural persons.

These participate in the money market just like natural persons, and they obviously have an unfair advantage. They don't get tired, hungry, thirsty, sleepy, or even old. Some of them specialize in "manufacturing" money, and lending it out to natural persons.

You have to be very careful and very smart

when you play the money game with these "people". A bank is a legal entity. It is not a human being. It will not get tired. It will not get old. But you will. Yes, it employs natural people, who get old and retire, and it employs more, who get old and retire, and so on and so forth. Even the CEO will get old and retire, and a new one will sit at the helm, and the process goes on.

So, you can't get emotional when you are playing the money game with an entity that has no emotions. You must seek to understand its language, and speak that language.

If, in the unlikely event that the bank should owe you - a natural person - money, it can just "manufacture" it and pay you off. I know that sounds very simplistic. But the fact that the bank can lend more money than it actually has, is proof that the bank can "manufacture" money. But that is a topic for another day.

For those interested in the banking system, there are many books on the subject, including *The Creature from Jekyll Island*[9],

---

[9] Griffin, G. Edward, 1994, The Creature from Jekyll Island, American Media

by Edward Griffin.
Now, back to the subject at hand.

The Necessity of Debt?

Is debt really that necessary? Can we really live without debt?

Banks and lending institutions have a big role to play in the development of our economies and societies. Without them rolling out debt, a lot of industrialists would not be able to innovate, invent, and improve lives.

Think of an industrialist like Henry Ford. If the banks did not advance him the money to build a motor manufacturing factory, we would still be walking or riding donkeys to work.

If the banks did not advance loans to General Electric, we would still be burning wood for light. If textile manufacturers had not borrowed money, we would still be running barefoot and topless. If there was no money lent to Microsoft, Apple and Google, we would still be whistling and shouting at each other to get each other's attention.

So yes, debt is necessary.

Without debt individuals would not be able to own homes at the rate that they can with debt. They would not be able to drive and own cars and furniture. They would not be able to pay for their children's education, which is an important investment in the future of their offspring.

When does debt go out of hand? Business debt goes wrong when it is given to incompetent entrepreneurs who confuse business money with personal money. Debt goes out of hand when it is given to people who cannot afford it. It goes out of hand when individuals start depending on it for survival. It goes out of hand when it is used for consumables like food and clothing. It goes out of hand when individuals use their houses like ATMs, cashing their equity for consumables. It goes wrong when there are no proper standards for measuring the adequacy of debt for each household.

It goes wrong when financial institutions are disconnected from each other and are not communicating with each other about each client. It would be good if they had a central system where they can check each client before they advance the money. Not just the credit bureau, which keeps a record of black listed people, but a system which can check the adequacy of debt per individual before the loans are advanced.

Generally, debt goes wrong in the hands of people who have no financial education, and cannot distinguish between their own money and other people's money, and their abilities to repay loans.

As long as we use money on our planet, debt is not going to disappear. It is too important for enabling developments. What we need therefore are better systems of managing debt. We need a financially educated society from business to individuals. We need legislation and supportive systems from government.

Yes, debt is important, but education about debt and money is even more important.

SELF-ASSESSMENT
1. What is the implication of using other people's money?
2. How do other players influence my money game?
3. What are the reasons that make debt necessary?
4. What would be the consequences if there was no debt?
5. When does debt go wrong?

CHAPTER 3

3. TOOLS OF CREDIT

The borrower is servant to the lender.
Proverbs 22:7

> LEARNING OUTCOMES
> In this chapter you will learn:
> 1. The difference between secured debt and unsecured debt.
> 2. Various tools of credit
> 3. The Use and misuse of tools of credit
> 4. The importance of credit life insurance

If you borrow money, and your goal is not to employ it but to consume it, then the proverb above applies. You have become a slave to the lender. You will work until you pay the last penny, including interest. If you fail, then your personal belongings will be sold to recover the debt.

Industrialists and business people don't borrow the bank's money to consume it, but to employ it. They speak the language of the bank. I believe if the bank had its way, it would only lend money to such people; people who would employ money. This guarantees the bank that it will get its money back.

The bank plays the game of the rich. It employs money. The most important employee of the bank, the hardest worker, is money; not the teller behind the counter, but the money in her hands. The teller draws a salary at the end of the month and is therefore an expense to the bank. The teller is dispensable, but not the cash. The bank's job is to send its money out to work and make more money for it.

If the bank could do everything through the Automated Teller Machine, they would do that. It would be cheaper for them.

The machine does not need a salary, it doesn't go on strike, and it does not take a coffee break, just regular maintenance is enough.

Now, the bank has created tools, or products, which it can sell to borrowers. The borrower is the garden on which the bank will plant its seed, hoping to reap a plentiful harvest. They will not plant their seed on barren land. You must learn to harness the power of debt.

Here are some of the tools of credit or products created by financial institutions for various clients:
1. Business loans
2. Mortgage loans
3. Personal loans
4. Short term asset loans (e.g. car loan/furniture)
5. Credit cards
6. Overdraft facilities

Let us explain them each briefly. Before we go into the explanations, let us understand the most important thing to a lender, before they lend their money out, is a certain level of certainty that they will be able to get their money back. This leads to secured loans and unsecured loans.

Secured vs. Unsecured Debt

What is Secured Debt?
Secured debt is debt that has collateral backing it up. This is a trade. The lender is willing to lend you money, but in the event that you fail to repay the loan, you have

some assets that they can take and sell and get their money back. You pledge these assets to the lender before they can give you a loan.

What is Unsecured Debt?
Unsecured debt is the opposite. This is a loan that has no collateral backing it up. When the bank talks of security, it is talking about its own security not yours. They feel secure if they lend money to someone who has assets, and they feel insecure if they are lending to someone who has no assets. To compensate for this insecurity, the bank charges the highest interest on unsecured loans.

Tools of Credit

Now let us look at each of the tools of credit:

1. **The Business Loan**
    A business loan is given to a business that can show through its business plan that it will generate the money to repay the loan. The business will get a secured loan if they have assets that they can pledge to the bank. In

the event that the business does not produce the revenues that allow it to service the loan, the bank can seize and sell the assets of the business to recover its money.

2. Mortgage Loan

A mortgage loan is a loan advanced to a person or company that wants to buy or build a piece of real estate property.

The property is mortgaged to the bank as security. If the borrower fails to pay, the bank can sell the piece of real estate to recover its money. This is a secured loan.

3. Personal Loans

Personal loans are unsecured loans based on the borrower's earning capabilities based mostly on employment. Your payslip gives you borrowing capacity. Since the lender depends on nothing else but your salary, they tend to charge a high interest for this facility.

The bank doesn't care what you use this money for. There is no particular asset attached to this loan. But don't assume that if you fail to pay the bank will not take your assets to sell.

4. Short Term Asset Finance Loans

Other secured loans include car loans and furniture loans based on the hire purchase scheme.

The car remains the bank's asset until you finish paying for it; just like the furniture on a hire-purchase scheme remain the property of the furniture shop until you finish paying for it.

5. Credit Cards

Credit cards are essentially the bank giving you a line of credit for a certain amount of time, usually two years. During this period, you may use the bank's money to the extent of your credit limit. Your responsibilities are to pay the minimum amounts as calculated by the bank.

What you have to remember about credit cards is that as long as you are only paying the minimum amounts, you will be charged interest on any remaining amount unpaid at the end of the month. If however, you pay off all that you have used up before the interest charging day, you will be using the bank's money for free. So, if you don't want to pay interest on your credit card, you should never carry a balance.

6. Overdraft Facilities

An overdraft facility is sort of like a credit card, except that you will be charged interest on any amount that you use, even if you pay it off the very next day. It is a line of credit. If you don't use it, you don't get charged any interest.

7. Store Cards

Store cards are essentially a line of credit extended to you by retailers. Most clothing retailers have store cards that give you a credit limit. You can take clothes, for example, on credit and pay them over time.

This is not free money. You will be charged interest on any outstanding balance.

If an item is only 100.00 bucks, please understand that if you take it on credit, the price will go up by the amount of interest you will be charged.

If goods are "on sale" and have been discounted by say 10%, if you take them on credit, and the interest is 20%, know that you will be paying 110% for them.

Credit Life Insurance

Most credit cards and almost all secured and unsecured debt come with credit life insurance. Credit life mostly covers events such as death. Should you die before the loan is repaid, the insurance company undertakes to pay off the loan.

Some credit life may cover life events such as disability, and retrenchment under certain conditions. Whenever you take a loan, read your credit life insurance policy to make sure you understand what is covered and what is not covered.

The Use and Misuse of Tools of Credit

Being educated about debt is critically important. When banks create loan packages, they are looking at matching your needs with their needs.

If you don't know much about debt, you can mix up the packages and use wrong products.

For example, if you use a personal loan to build or buy a house, you are using a wrong product for your needs. The interest for a personal loan is very high because by its nature, a personal loan is an unsecured debt. The interest for a mortgage loan is low because the house is used as security.

It therefore does not make economic sense to use a very expensive personal loan to finance the building of a house, which you could have financed with cheap mortgage loan.

It further does not make economic sense to roll off personal loans and car loans into your mortgage through the process called debt consolidation.

Match your project needs with the right kind of debt.

Is Cash King?

Many financial teachers or advisors would have you believe that it is best to be a cash buyer and stay away from debt. And perhaps they are right. For a lot of people, operating a cash system has kept them out of unnecessary heartaches, and many more would do well to try the cash-is-king system.

However, without debt, many desires would go unfulfilled. Some people feel they can't save up for 20 years to buy a house or for 5 years to buy a car. Debt allows them to have these things now. So, if it's available, and you can afford it, why not?

There are no right or wrong answers. There are only preferences. Whatever preferences you choose, be informed about them, and be well conversant with how they work. It is not the availability of debt that is a problem, it is the management of debt that gives people a lot of problems. It is important to have the guidance of a trained financial advisor to go through your specific situation. In the next chapter we begin to look at the building blocks of debt, the four elements of debt.

SELF-ASSESSMENT
1. What is the difference between secured debt and unsecured debt?
2. List at least five tools of credit?
3. Which of the tools of credit are most important to you and why?
4. What is the importance of credit life insurance?
5. How do consumers misuse tools of credit?

Nelson Letshwene

CHAPTER 4

4. THE FOUR ELEMENTS OF DEBT

"Never spend your money before you have earned it."

Thomas Jefferson

> LEARNING OUTCOMES
>
> In this chapter you will learn;
>
> 1. The four elements of debt
> 2. The importance of co-ordinating the four elements of debt
> 3. The effects of isolating each of the elements of debt

Let us start by understanding the four very

important elements of debt. Every loan or credit that you have taken is characterised by four elements: the principal amount, the instalment, interest, and time. These factors are inextricably intertwined and each one of them affects the others.

An increase in one of them affects the others, and a decrease in any one affects all the others. None of these are independent of each other. The danger that face borrowers is that they don't see the relationship of each of these factors to each other, and as a result, treat them as separate entities. Let us look at each one of them at a time.

1. The Loan Amount

The loan amount is the total amount that you will owe the lender at the start of the loan. This is not to be confused with the amount that you receive in your account. The amount you receive in your account may be increased by administration fees; credit life insurance; initiation fees; and whatever other fees your lender may charge you to arrive at the total amount of the loan.

Once the additional charges are computed, they are added to the amount you receive, then interest is computed, to formulate the total amount owed.

If, for an example, you want to borrow 50'000, the total amount you owe will be affected by all the other factors.

If all additional fees come to say, 5'000, you will only receive 45'000 in your account.

If the *interest rate is 10% per annum compounded monthly over 2 years*, your instalments over the period will be 2'307.25.

You can see that if you multiplied your instalment amount by 24 months, you get 55'373.91. This is the total amount being owed.

You only got 45'000 in your account, but you will sign that you owe the lender 55'373.91.

Most borrowers don't think about anything else. All they want to know is: how much is coming into my hands right now.

2. The Instalment Amount

The next important thing that most borrowers worry about is, how much are the monthly instalments.

They are not looking at the total amount that the series of instalments will amount to. They only want to know if they can afford it this month!

Making a commitment today that has long term repercussions that you don't consider, is dangerous.

A person who is only worried about instalments, may say to the lender, please make my instalments easier.

In the above example, they might say, I can't afford to pay 2'307,91.

To make it "affordable", the lender might reduce instalments to 1'268,13. This might make the borrower happy. But the only way to reduce instalments to this level is to increase time to 4 years or 48 months. Now, multiplying the 1'268,13 by 48 months makes the loan amount 60'870,20. You still only get 45'000 in your account, but your will repay a total of 60'870,20, which is 15'870,20 more! This happens when you only focus on instalments.

It is obviously very important to make sure that you can afford your instalments, but it is vitally important that you think about the whole picture.
The lower your instalments are, the longer you will take to repay the debt. The longer you take, the higher your principal debt.

3. Interest

Interest is the price you pay for borrowed money. Most borrowers have no clue what this really means. They understand the amount of the loan that is coming into their account, and they also understand the instalments they will pay every month. They however, have no clue how the concept called interest plays a role.
This is why most people can't differentiate between a loan taken from a bank and a loan taken from cash loan or loan sharks.
While the bank will quote their interest using annual rate, the loan shark uses monthly rate. An annual rate of 20% at the bank, and a monthly rate of 20% at the loan

shark seem to be the same to an untrained and desperate borrower.

The bank's annual rate will most like be compounded monthly, which, in simplistic terms, means the 20% per annum will be divided by 12 months to give you a monthly rate of 1.67%.

Now, comparing this with the loan shark who will be charging the full 20% every month, where should you really go to go borrow money?

If you just multiplied the loan shark's 20% by 12 months, you will see that you are paying 240% per annum.

Each time you take a loan, consider the price you are paying for the loan. Money is not free. Money is sold in the money market at a price. You should get the most competitive price possible for your money.

When the bank says, "you qualify" for a loan, they are not doing you a favour. They are also looking for a customer. You don't have to sign on the spot. It is important that you should shop around and find the most affordable interest that you can afford.

There is nothing wrong with getting several quotations from several lenders to compare the terms before you make your decision.

People who go to loan sharks often say they

do so because they don't qualify at the bank. Here is what does not make sense: if you don't qualify at the bank where the interest rates are lower, why would you take money where it is most expensive?

And the answer is, I'm under pressure. I need the money now.

Don't allow desperation to lead you into the most expensive loans. Remember, this is other people's money, and it comes at a price. Don't be in a hurry to take other people's money without considering what it will cost you.

4. Time

Time is a very fleeting factor in debt management and most people don't give it a second thought because they can't see it.

But by just looking at the example we used above, see what the difference in the loan amount is between a loan that is repaid in 2 years (24 months) and a loan that is repaid in 4 years (48 months).

Most people who consolidate their loans or do "top ups" only think about the pressure of the Instalment amount, and do not consider time or the interest rate.

Sometimes they only see the pressure of the problem in front of them that requires money. They go and borrow money to solve the "big" problem in front of them that require money, without considering that they are giving birth to an even bigger problem that will take years to resolve. Before you ever take a loan, think about these four elements of debt and how they will affect you.

Debt restructuring often focuses on reducing your instalments. But you must remember, for instalments to go down, it means time must go up. When time goes up, the principal amount goes up, simply because you will be paying your interest for longer.

SELF-ASSESSMENT

1. What are the four elements of debt?
2. Explain how each of the four elements of debt play a role in the composition of debt
3. What are the effects of isolating the four elements of debt from each other?
4. What happens if you only focus on reducing the monthly instalment to a loan?

Nelson Letshwene

CHAPTER 5

5. THE GAP PLANNING SYSTEM

"When a man is in love or in debt, someone else has the advantage."
Bill Balance

> LEARNING OUTCOMES
>
> In this chapter you will learn:
>
> 1. How to set up a planning structure
> 2. The importance of protection in your structure

In order to follow this Financial Planning System that I suggest, it would be important to have your income statement and balance sheet in front of you so that you know what you are dealing with. The key with a planning system is that it must propel you forward instead of holding you at the same place or worse, taking you back.

The Flow of Your Money

Now you must determine the flow of your cash. What happens to money when it arrives into your system?

You need to watch it so that you can make decisions and perhaps redirect the flow of your cash if it is going the wrong way.

For most people, unfortunately the money does not even arrive into their hands. The pay-slip shows that the money gets taken from the employer by their creditors and only very little makes it to their pockets. So, they really have no control over the flow of their cash.

For other people, whereas the pay-slip may show that they get most of their money from the employer, the bank statement will show that the direct debits on their accounts are like blood suckers and they are still broke at the end of the pay period.

The Suggested Plan

Note that this is only a suggestion. You need to find what would work for you.

Now, the Planning System is based on a suggested 10:10:20:60 system. This is only a suggestion depending where you are at. If you can't apply this right away, you can make it your goal to achieve in a set period of time. It is important to save 10% of your earnings. If you can't, keep making adjustments to your life until you reach this goal. You do the same with all the other allocations as explained below.

- The first 10% should go to Paying Yourself First. This money goes in an account and is not taken out until you are ready to invest it. A savings account is not necessarily an investment account. By investment I mean things like the money market, the stock market, real estate, your business, etc. This that will actually bring a return back.
- The second 10% should at least go to Protection. Protection makes sure that the assets you are gathering are not exposed to vulnerabilities. If you have finished paying for your home, make sure you get homeowner insurance. This

will protect your house against fire or other damages like a leaking geyser. If you don't have this cover, you might find yourself having to start over. Make sure all your assets are well insured. You should also have a good life insurance policy, Retirement annuity, and a rainy-day reserve or emergency fund

- Failure to have adequate life insurance can leave you in a desperate position should anything drastic happen. Some people claim they can't afford life insurance, but I believe that especially if you can't afford it, then you can't afford to be without it. Dealing with financial problems without a good life insurance cover is like going to war without protection.
- The next 20% of your income should be what is used to cover all your debts. You might be saying that is not possible! Pay attention for a while here. Take a list of all your debts and decide that you will only apply 20% of your income to repay them. Yes, this means you will have to call them and make new arrangements if you are already using much more than 20% to service debt. If this is not immediately possible, make it your goal

to cut your debt servicing amount to only 20% or less. Take control of your cash flow. We will look at different methods in the next chapter.
- We allocate 60% to your current living expenses because it is important that you do not get in any more debt. You should be able to live without borrowing from the first day to the last day of the month. Most people stay in debt because they don't allocate enough of their own money to themselves. So, they are always dependent on debt for survival. To close the door on debt starts with you not entering that door ever again.

If you can do this, you are on your way out of trouble. Avoid another "survival-till-end-of-the-month" loan.

That is why you need to allocate enough of your money to avoid the "lend-me-I'll-pay-at-month-end" syndrome.

It is worth emphasizing that if you want to get out of debt and start building a nest egg, it is important that you don't continue to get into any more debt – even if it is short term (especially unsecured debt).

You need to banish the idea and find other

ways to survive. Rather increase your means. Review the chapter on The Money Trees and see how else you can make more money.

SELF-ASSESSMENT

1. Describe the 10:10:20:60 planning system
2. What is the importance of protection?
3. How can you make sure you stay out of debt?

Chapter 6

6. DEBT STRATEGIES

"Every time you borrow money, you're robbing your future self."
Nathan W. Morris

LEARNING OUTCOMES
In this chapter you will learn the following ways of DEBT REDUCTION:
- Urgent Debt
- Costly Debt
- Debt Consolidation
- Size of Debt
- How to communicate with creditors

When you are in debt beyond your limit, you need to do something to rescue yourself. Being overly indebted means more of your current income is going towards servicing debt, to the extent that you have little to live on. This forces you to keep borrowing just to survive. Being overly indebted also means after paying your instalments and your living expenses, you have nothing left to save. You seem to be in balance, but you are not creating a future at all.

There are a number of things you will have to do to address this.

First, make a list of all your debts, and I mean all of them, both formal and informal. We are going to look at this list from different angles, depending on how it is affecting you. Once you have this list, comb through it to determine which debts can be classified as very urgent.

Urgent Debt

Urgency is defined by asking this question: "which debt, if not paid now, is likely to cause you the most trouble?" Trouble can be defined as being black listed by the credit bureau, facing legal proceedings, facing debt collection, or facing repossession of your goods, etc. Debt becomes urgent when you neglect or are unable to make regular scheduled payments.

By separating your most urgent debt from normal debt that's on schedule, it helps you to identify the trouble spots in your relationship with debt.

It does not necessarily mean you are going to clear or pay off every debt on this sub-list. This allows you to formulate a strategy to deal with these, without neglecting the others.

The problem with urgent debt is that it may cause panic, and when people panic, they may make rushed decisions, which they might regret later.

You may need to start talking to these creditors first in order to take away your panic. If they are already too upset because you have ignored them for too long, you still need to approach them and make a new offer.

It doesn't help you to rush and take another loan to pay off these urgent debts, because this new loan will be tomorrow's emergency.

Your strategy for dealing with urgent debt may include:

- Consulting with a debt counsellor to help you think through this and come up with a new plan.

- It will invariably include talking to your creditors and perhaps coming up with a new payment plan.
- It may include an assessment of some of your assets to see which you could sell to repay this debt.
- It may include a plan to make more money through an additional income stream that will be focused on repaying the arrears and eventually paying off these debts.
- It should NOT include taking another loan, unless under the advice of a trained professional. Another loan is feasible only if that loan will help you to make more money, as in a business loan. But you should not take another loan that will also depend on your salary. Don't consolidate yet. (We will talk about debt consolidation later in this chapter).

Once your most urgent debt is taken care of, that is, you have a plan for it, you should stick to your plan, and not let the other debts fall behind.

If none of your debt will put you in immediate danger, that is, you have no urgent debt, consider the next criteria of dealing with debt.

The Cost of Debt

One of the things people don't always think about is the cost of debt. There is no such thing as a free lunch. Debt comes at a cost. Now you need to arrange your debt in order, following the price of debt.

Go through your list again asking yourself: "which debts carries the highest interest charge?"

As discussed in the chapter on the four elements of debt, pay attention to the compounding interest rate. By listing your debts according to the price, you pay for your money, it helps you to figure out which debt you should try to eliminate first and save money.

A rough guide to costs in descending order would be:
- Cash loans
- Loans from micro-lenders;
- Hire-purchase agreements;
- Credit cards;
- Personal loans;

- Overdraft facilities;
- Vehicle loans;
- Mortgage bonds;
- Interest free loan from your uncle.

The above order is not cast in stone, and thus may not be true for you. You need to establish from your own records as to which debts cost you the most.

You can then devise a strategy for dealing with the most expensive debt first. With this method, you try to pay off the debt which costs you the most to have.

Unfortunately, many advisors have used this method to advice clients to roll their most expensive unsecured consumer debt into their mortgage debt.

This is a mistake because you end up paying off consumer debt over a very long period. Whatever you do, don't forget the four elements of debt.

Just because your personal loan is 30% per annum and your home loan is 11% per annum, does not mean you will reduce interest by rolling your personal loan into your home loan. If you roll your personal loan into your mortgage loan, it means you will be paying your personal loan over 25 years, or the length of your mortgage. It doesn't make sense to pay for consumables for that long. This also delays you from owning your home.

Most people, after clearing their credit card debt or personal loans into their mortgage loan, get "tempted" to use that "clean" credit card again. The lenders whose accounts have been paid off also make new offers, and people go and take another personal loan. Their situation does not improve. As we discussed under urgent debt, you can utilize anyone of those strategies to come up with extra cash to deal with your most expensive debt.

Debt Consolidation

The most frequently used methodology for dealing with debt is the Debt Consolidation method. Most debt counsellors and financiers resort to this method in dealing with debt.

It is vitally important to make sure you know what you are doing before you engage this method.

Debt consolidation basically means you are going to borrow new money, to pay off old loans.

Why would you want to do this?
The greatest motivation for people consolidating their debt is to reduce the amount of the instalments they are paying. They also think they want to reduce the number of creditors they owe.

How does this work?
Most people look at the list of instalments they have to pay each month. They add up the total amounts of the instalments. They then focus on reducing the instalments. They generally don't think about the total debt. Just the instalments.

A debt consolidator's selling point is that you don't have to owe so many creditors. The borrower takes a fresh loan from the lender, with the goal of getting rid of all other creditors. The borrower often feels better that they only owe one creditor, instead of many.

CAUTION: The problem with this method is that IF you have not yet taken care of the habits that got you into this mess, you are very likely to get into a bigger mess than before. Many people who use their mortgage loans to consolidate their credit cards and other loans can testify to going right back to using the credit card again, or applying for a fresh personal loan.

For, as soon as your account is paid up at ABC123 Stores, you might receive a letter praising you for being such a good customer, and offering you more debt, and you might be worse off at the end. Use this method of Debt Consolidation only if you have the discipline to *not* get back into the spiral again.

Having someone you are accountable to and you discuss your finances with, might help you to stay rational, especially when those tempting offers come to you again.

Don't forget the 4 elements of debt!

When applying this method, please do not forget the four elements of debt. This is where the biggest mistakes are made. It doesn't help you to trade a cheap loan for an expensive loan.

If you don't consider interest rates and just consolidate because the lender said you qualify, you might find yourself trading a loan that you took at a lower interest rate a year or two ago, for a much more expensive loan at today's interest rates.

If you don't consider time, you could be consolidating a loan that is left with six months into a loan that will go for sixty months. Extending the time of a loan increases the amount you will repay.

Remember that debt consolidation means you are taking a fresh loan with new terms and conditions. You are selling off your "old" loans to the "new" lender. He pays off your old debt and you commit to him for another full term.

What is Debt Restructuring?

Debt restructuring is similar to debt consolidation, except in debt restructuring, you don't necessarily have to take a new loan.

You approach the current creditors and negotiate new terms with them.

If you desire to reduce the instalments you are paying, your time will obviously go up, which will affect the final amount that you owe.

You can also ask to increase the amount of your instalments. This will decrease the time you will take to repay the loan, with the effect that your principal debt is reduced.

If you should come into some extra money, or create an additional stream of income, you can use this to increase your instalments, which will get you out of debt faster. Let us now look into how to create a debt management plan.

SELF-ASSESSMENT
1. What is the criteria for classifying debt as urgent debt?
2. What strategies can you employ to deal with urgent debt?
3. How do you determine the cost of your debt?
4. What is debt consolidation?
5. How should you apply the four elements of debt when you are consolidating debt?

Chapter 7

7. DEBT MANAGEMENT PLAN

"If a man works hard, the land will not be lazy"
Chinese proverb

> LEARNING OUTCOMES
> In this chapter you will learn:
> 1. The size of debt method
> 2. Timing in dealing with debt
> 3. The importance of communicating with your creditors

The idea of managing debt is about creating a system that will guide you either out of debt, or into using debt in a way that fits in with your overall financial strategy.

A debt management plan is not a plan that seems to get you out of debt overnight. It is a system that you should follow and manage over time. The best way to deal with debt is to create a strategy and implement this strategy.

Even if you are overly indebted right now, you need a strategy that will get you out of debt, and keep you out of debt. As long as you are working with debt, you are working with other people's money. The way to success in the financial game is to make sure you are growing your own money, not someone else's.

Let us look at a strategy that could help us to eliminate debt.

The Size of Debt Method

Go through that list of debt and now rearrange it according to size, from the smallest to the biggest debt. Size can be determined in two ways: either in terms of the real balance on the loan, or the amount of time left to pay off the loan.

If you follow the balance method, then you just list your debts looking at the total amount owed to each creditor.

CREDITOR	BALANCE
PAUL	1'000
PETER	3'000
MARY	5'000
ABC	10'000

If you make extra money, you use it to pay off Paul, so that you reduce the number of creditors you have.

Let us not forget that each debt is governed by the four elements of debt. Now let us look at the instalments applied to each of these, as well as the time left on each loan.

Let us assume that your smallest balance is the one with the shortest amount of time.

In other words, if you owe say 1'000 to one creditor and 5'000 to another, depending on the instalments to each, we assume that the smallest amount could be paid off first or in the shortest amount of time.

CREDITOR	BALANCE	INSTALL-MENT	TIME
PAUL	1'000	200	5 months
PETER	3'000	300	10
MARY	5'000	330	15
ABC	10'000	500	20

What this means is, in your spread sheet, slot in all the minimum payments required in each of your debts from the smallest debt to the biggest.

When you finish paying your smallest debt in five months' time as per the schedule above, instead of using that amount that used to go to your smallest debt to increase your expenses, you apply that amount in addition to your next smallest debt, which, in this case, would be to Peter.

This means you are now paying minimum debt on all your debts, except now with your current smallest debt, you are paying an additional amount, which is what you used to pay to your previous smallest debt.

In other words, even if you finish paying any of your debts as per your list, you don't change your debt ratio. If had decided that you will apply 20% of your income towards debt, you keep applying 20% of your income to debt until all your debt is paid off. All you do is you keep adjusting the amount payable to the smallest debt on your list. This encourages you as you see the list of your creditors decreasing.

Using Time as a criterion

The length of time you will take is determined by the instalments you are paying.

Obviously if your instalments to the 5'000 is 2'500 per month and your instalments to the 1'000 debt is 150 per month, you will take longer to pay off the 1'000 than you would the 5'000. So, it will take you only two instalments to get you out of the 5'000 debt and almost seven months to get you out of the 1'000 debt.

Whichever criteria you use, whether balance in amount or in time, we're trying to get you out of this debt as quickly as possible. That is the goal.

As soon as you pay off the 5'000 loan in two months, you could immediately, in the third month, clear off the balance of the 1'000 loan with the instalment that used to go to the 5'000 loan.

This is one of the most effective methods when used to eliminate debt. Listing them this way helps you to pay the smallest debt first, then using the instalment of the just cleared debt to tackle the next smallest, and so on.

Let's consider the example below:

What if you could make extra money?

If you can come up with an extra 100.00 say either from your budget or from one of your other skills preferably, then you add the 100.00 to the payment that is being made to the smallest debt on your list, which in the table below is to Paul.

CREDITOR	BALANCE	INSTALL-MENT	TIME	NEW TIME
PAUL	1'000	200	5 months	3.1
PETER	3'000	300	10	7 (3.5)
MARY	5'000	330	15	9 (3)
ABC	10'000	500	20	11 (4)

So, instead of paying Paul 200.00 and taking 5 months to repay him, you give him 300.00 and you pay him off in about 3 months.

You then take the 300.00 (that is, the 200.00 that used to go to Paul plus the new 100.00 that you are making from your other skills) and now apply it to the next smallest debt on your list, which is a debt to Peter.

Since you'd been paying Peter his minimum payment of 300.00 over the past three months, by the time you come with an extra

300.00, there will be 7 months left in his debt. You now pay Peter 600.00 instead of 300.00. In 3.5 months you shall have cleared his debt, instead of the 7 months it would have taken, had you continued to pay only the minimum payment.

You now have access to an additional 600.00 that you can apply to your next smallest debt, which is Mary. By giving Mary 930.00 instead of 330.00 you get to pay her off in 3 months, saving yourself 6 months. You keep this up until you clear your entire list of debts.

If you focus only on the big debts, by the time you finish paying them, your smaller debts may have grown to bigger debts, or your uncle may not want to see you again. Tackling the smaller debts will free the money quickly for you to start going after the big ones. The size method is my most preferred method of debt clearance, and if applied diligently, can free you from debt in a shorter amount of time than the other methods.

Commit to Your Why

If you are not committed to your WHY, you

will get back into the spiral. If you don't have a big enough reason to get out of debt and start building your financial future, you may get stuck in this habit again. It is important that you don't just want to get out of debt just for the sake of getting out of debt, you need to do it with your eye on a bigger goal. Set a vision of your future self.

Talk to Your Creditors

For any of these methods to work well however, you will have to do this seemingly daunting task: Talk to your creditors!

Creditors have better memories than debtors. Your creditors actually would like to talk to you. The reasonable ones do not mind renegotiating the terms.
Why? Well, it's certainly not because they like you or are having pity for you. They are thinking about themselves: if they can come up with a payment plan that you can afford, they are more likely to get some or all of their money back, than if they can't get hold of you.
So don't run away, run towards them. If you are quiet, your creditors are also afraid that

you will run away with their money. So they are likely to get you in trouble. They will go to the lawyers or to debt collectors, or get you black listed with the credit bureau. And believe me, one of the assets you need to protect is your credit rating.

If you are really in trouble, be sensible and make an offer to your creditors. If they are sensible, and most are, (though sadly not all), they will accept your offer, albeit grudgingly.

Here is a sample letter you might want to send off to your creditors. But don't just send the letter and keep quiet. This sample letter is only one of the tools you might use to deal with your debt, not the answer to all your creditors. Here is the sample letter

Letter to Creditors

To: _____

Dear Sir/Madam

RE: Account number: _____

This serves as an acknowledgment of my indebtedness to you to the amount of
_____

I intend to repay my full debt to you. I write to inform you that I have reviewed all my debts and after seeking advice and counselling, have come up with a repayment schedule. This will help me to fulfil my obligations to you in a way that will put me in a stable financial position.

To this end, I have created a Debt Clearance Account, made up of twenty per cent of my regular income. The purpose of this is to allow me to have sufficient resources to live on without worry or stress, and it will prevent me from going further into debt.

I am aware that as long as I continue to live on borrowed money, I don't stand a chance of ever getting out of debt and stabilizing my financial position. Each month, you will receive an amount of _____ from my Debt Clearance system until my account with you is cleared.

I am aware that this is not the amount I had previously agreed to pay you, but I'm sure you will be understanding and appreciate what I am doing. If you have any questions, please feel free to contact me. I am quite excited about my new plans and look forward to taking control of my finances.

Thank you in advance for your kind cooperation.

Yours truly, _____

SELF-ASSESSMENT
1. What is the size of debt method and how does it work?
2. How do you prioritize debt based on time remaining?
3. What is the importance of making extra income in dealing with debt?
4. Why is commitment so important?
5. Why is it important to communicate with your creditors?

Chapter 8

8. THE STATE WE'RE IN

"Debt is an opportunity for the rich"
Unknown

Most people are very much in the dark when it comes to debt. They have too much of it, and the wrong kinds. They strip their homes of equity and bounce balances from credit card to credit card to fuel their overspending. They think that because a lender is willing to give them money, they can afford to pay it back.

They focus on small things like monthly payments rather than the big picture of how the wrong kind of debt is a cancer eating away at their financial security. They pay interest year after year, enriching lenders while stealthily, silently, impoverishing themselves. And they wonder why they never seem to get ahead.

Money can buy slavery or freedom, you choose what you buy with your money. It can buy flexibility and independence, or a prison cell. Many people have rightly observed that no matter what they do, they don't seem to be able to get out from under. They try for several months, and once again, they find themselves right where they began. Some even pay off all their debt, but then find themselves in more debt in no time.

Is it that debt is impossible to live without or is there some magnetic pull that draws us in subconsciously?

Debt is like an addiction. One of the most effective organisations in getting people off the hook of a grossly debilitating condition of addiction is the Alcoholics Anonymous (AA) organization. Over decades now people have been able to recover from their addictions. What is the secret that the AA uses?

The AA has discovered the secret to helping people get off booze. They recognise that addiction is a spiritual problem. One of the most profound statements they make is that an addict will never be able to recover from his addiction until he changes his personality.

All human behaviours come from our beliefs. Our beliefs sponsor our behaviours. Until you are willing to sit down and examine the beliefs you hold about money and debt, you don't stand a chance of permanent recovery from debt.

You may have many temporary recoveries over your life but a permanent recovery, which can catapult you above debt and set you in control, thus enabling you to be able to use debt to your advantage, will take your willingness to deal with your beliefs about money.

Most people never get this message. As soon as they get a job, or even before that, they get a credit card.

Instead of saving and investing, they buy stuff - usually stuff that doesn't last as long as the payments on it. If they manage to contribute to a savings or retirement policy, they either borrow from it or cash it out when they change jobs.

As their homes increase in value, they take out home-equity loans - offsetting most or the entire potential rise in their wealth with more debt.

The percentage of disposable income used to make debt payments is now near an all-time high. The number of bankruptcies keeps setting records, with millions of people worldwide going bankrupt. Foreclosures are at modern highs, and the number of home loans more than 30 days overdue is rising.

It would be naïve to lay all the blame at the feet of consumers. Lenders have done their part by loosening loan standards and chasing after people with poor credit in an ill-fated attempt to boost their profits.

Credit-card companies ferociously battle efforts to help debtors see the hole they're digging, saying it would be "too difficult" to spell out for individual customers how long it would take to pay off their balances if only minimum payments are made.

But on a personal level, it's pointless to blame the rope salesman for selling you rope, if you use it to hang yourself. Once you've tied the noose, it's up to you to undo the knot.

Michael Masterson, author of *Automatic Wealth* wrote:

"Acknowledging and repaying your debts - these are two very fundamental requirements of integrity.

You must acknowledge your debt because it is your chance to honour your creditor. And you must repay your debt because it is your chance to honour yourself."

Nelson Letshwene

Appendix A

Q & A on Dealing with Personal Debt

The following answers to questions should only be regarded as a general guide and not personal advice. For a more specific advice, it would be very important to consult with a financial advisor to look at your specific situation and numbers. These however give a general understanding on some of the issues covered.

General Debt Questions

1. **I Can I Borrow Money to Buy Shares?**
   Yes and no. You can borrow money for anything you want. Whether or not it's a good idea to buy with the sole purpose of buying shares is another issue. The banks will not use your future shares as collateral - so the loan will be a personal loan. If you make a loss, they will not share your losses with you, you still have to pay them everything you owe them. If

you make a profit they will also not demand your profits. So, you see, you are on our own.

2. How Does Interest Rate Affect My Loan?

Interest is the price you pay for borrowed money. It is very important to examine how this price is calculated so that you know exactly how much you are paying for your loan. There is simple interest and compound interest. They are calculated differently, and the answers will amount to different figures. The calculation of interest is also always based on the amount of time associated with your loan. This is referred to as the compounding period. Short compounding periods increases the frequency of the calculations.

3. How Does the Loan Term Affect My Loan?

- The loan term is the period over which you will repay your loan
- The longer the period, the more time the lender has to charge you interest
- The shorter the period, the shorter you have to pay interest
- The loan term will only be altered if you changed your instalment amount.
- If you increased your instalments, it will be shorter, thus saving you interest
- If you decreased your instalment, it will be longer, thus increasing the amount you owe

- When you are consolidating a loan, or doing a top-up, you are actually cancelling the old loan and starting anew one with a new loan term.
- Pay attention to your loan term because it affects the amount of money you will pay

4. How Does a Consolidation Loan Work?

- A consolidation loan is a loan you take and use to pay other loans you already have
- Most people use a consolidation loan to reduce the total amount of instalments that they pay
- By focusing only on the instalments, they take their eyes off of the amount of debt they are getting into, and they pay no attention to the amount of time they will be in debt
- Most people don't just take the amount of loan equal to the debt that they have, they take a bigger loan than the debts that they have so that they can have additional cash in their hands
- That additional cash increases the amount of their indebtedness
- Before you take a consolidation loan, it would be a good idea to meet with a financial advisor and look purely at the

numbers and their long-term implications.

5. What Are Some Advantages and Disadvantages of Debt Consolidation?

- The immediate advantage is the reduction in your instalment amount
- If you had been overcommitted, this relief can help you to rearrange your finances and take charge again
- The purpose of a consolidation loan should be to stop any other loans, especially pay-day loans that you used to survive from pay-cheque to pay-cheque
- Since your instalments get "normalised", you should not have to take another pay-day loan for survival.
- Debt consolidation should therefore only be used with the guidance of a financial advisor, and with determined financial discipline on your side.
- **The DISADVANTAGES** are that a consolidation loan increases the amount of time you will remain in debt.
- There is also the temptation to take another loan since you have a breather in your finances
- It is also important not to consolidate smaller short-term loan using the equity in your home. Don't make your house

an ATM. If you do, you will end up paying for smaller things over the term of the mortgage, which is not good financial planning

6. How Does a Change (Reduction/Increase) of My Instalment Amount Affect My Loan?

- Here you have to remember that every loan has 4 elements, and instalment is only just one of the four elements (The others are Interest, Time, and of course the Principal amount)
- Any change in any of the four elements will affect the others
- A reduction in your instalments, is made possible by an extension in the time of the loan, or technically, the starting over of a new loan term all together, as happens when you take a consolidation loan.
- By increasing the time of the loan, you are giving interest an extra time to be charged to your principal, thus increasing your total indebtedness
- An increase in your instalment works in your favour in that it reduces the amount of time, and consequently, the total amount of debt you will repay.

7. What Is Credit Life Insurance and Its Benefits?

- Credit life insurance is an insurance policy that accompanies your loan at the bank
- It is automatically ceded to the bank and will cover the balance in your loan should you die before you finish paying off your loan
- This is a product initiated by the bank for the safety of the bank, but you get to pay the premiums on it for the duration of the loan
- If your employer is acting as a guarantor on your loan, that is, you are part of a guaranteed scheme, then credit life insurance should not be necessary, unless such things as retrenchments are not included in the policy
- So, it is important to read this policy since you are the one who is paying for it, and it is important to let your loved ones know that should you die, the loan should "settle itself" through this policy, and the lender should not go to the employer to take your benefits for the loan
- When you take a mortgage loan, it is important to also have a credit life cover, to ensure that your loved ones don't lose the house to the lender, should you die.

Credit Cards

8. What Is the Structure of a Credit Card?
- A credit card is essentially three loans in one
- The straight credit is that which is available as "free money" for 55 days
    - That means from the date of purchase or swiping your card, you should not be charged interest for 55 days
    - If you paid within that 55-day period, you shall have had access to free money
- The budget facility is an instalment purchase system within the credit card
    - Whatever you charge to your budget facility, you are allowed to pay over the period that you choose, from 6 months
- Cash advance from an ATM is a loan you take from your credit card
    - If you withdraw money from your credit card, you are essentially taking a loan from the bank

9. When Do I Get Charged Interest on My Credit Card? (Technical!!!)

- Depending on which of the facilities available on your credit card you have used, you will be charged differently
- Your straight balance does not attract interest for 55 days from the date of first usage, and technically for every 55 days from each swiping point or purchases point per transaction.
- If you don't clear your balance at the end of the month, chances are you will be caught up with interest at some point
- The purchases that go on your budget are immediately charged interest based on the term that you have chosen. There is no 55 days grace on that one.
- You will immediately be shown your total budget balance, and the instalments that will be added to your straight balance, and thus being available for clearing at the end of the month.
- If you don't clear your balance at the end of the month, and therein is your budget instalment as well, you must understand that your budget instalment will also be charged interest again, this time with the interest of the straight facility
- Cash advances at the ATM are loans and are charged immediately. They are

not available for 55 days as free money.
- Cash advances will immediately reduce your straight balance, but they get charged interest immediately

10. How Does the Budget Facility on My Credit Card Work?

- The budget facility on your credit card is tantamount to an instalment sale transaction, except you don't have to fill in hire-purchase forms at the store, you already have the facility on your credit card
- You need to see these in the same light that you would a hire-purchase agreement
- If you want a big-ticket item but you don't have the money to buy it cash, you can buy it using your budget facility and pay it over the time period you choose from 6 months to maybe 48 months
- At the end of every month, the instalment amount is added to your straight balance and is available for clearance that month
- This will carry on until you finish paying the budget balance.
- Each month that you pay the instalment, that same instalment

- amount becomes available again in your budget balance
- So, you budget facility is part of the revolving credit, just as your straight balance is

11. What Is the Best Way to Manage and Deal with The Balance on My Credit Card?

- Managing a credit card is a matter of financial planning and financial discipline
- Because it is a revolving credit system, it is easy to not see it as debt, because every time you pay the debt, it becomes available again
- The best way to deal with a credit card is to clear the balance at the end of every month.
- If you only pay the minimum amount, you will be charged fees and interest on your balance
- It is also only better to use your credit card as available for emergencies, but not as something that you start depending on the revolving nature of the debt
- Cutting up your credit cards does not make the debt disappear, but yes it may stop you from using the physical card, even though you can still shop on line as long as you know the numbers

12. Why Do They Want Me to Pay So Little on My Credit Card?

- The required minimum payment on your credit card is not the instalment of the credit card, it is the minimum you need to pay to avoid going into default
- If you never use your credit card but only pay the minimum, you will notice that the minimum required keeps dropping each month
- If you want to pay off your credit card, you need to pay more than the minimum required on your statement,
- If you don't pay the required for one month, you might notice that the minimum doubles, and the credit card company can suspend your credit,
- That is because you have gone into default

13. Should I Include My Credit Card Debt When I Consolidate?

- We have spoken about consolidation processes before
- Whether or not to include your credit card in your consolidation plans depends what your intentions are
- If you intend to pay it off and never use it again, then it's probably not a bad

- idea since credit cards carry a higher interest rates than other debt
- If however, clearing it would be creating another opportunity for you to use it, thus going further into debt, then you have to decide whether what you want to use it for is worth it or not
- It would not be a good idea to clear it only to use it further for consumption spending.
- Consolidating a credit card balance into a longer-term loan means everything you bought by that credit card is now being paid over a longer period of time

Cash Loans

14. What Is the Difference Between Formal and Informal Loans?

- There are many differences, and one of the differences is in the vetting processes
- There is usually no vetting process to get an informal loan, so you get it just for asking
- The formal loans go through a vetting process that allows you to consider whether you should get the loan or not

- The administration is also different in that there will be more formal communication with a formal loan than there would be with an informal loan
- The way the interest is calculated makes a huge difference in the pricing of these loans
    o Formal loans give you the interest rate per annum, charged monthly, which makes them generally cheaper
    o Informal loans charge you simple interest per month, and it gets compounded monthly, which makes them very expensive
- Because a formal loan follows standard pricing models, you can predict what you would owe at the end of the loan
- Informal loans can fluctuate with just one missed instalment
- Formal loans can identify how much is in arrears and you can be given an opportunity to deal with the arrears properly
- Informal loans don't separate the arrears from the normal loan, all is lumped together and can be overwhelming

15. Why Is Revolving Debt, Such as Overdraft Facilities, Credit Cards, and Cash Loans So Addictive?

- The addiction of these debts is because of the fact that they create a dependency syndrome
- Revolving debts are like a bottomless pit
- As soon as you pay an instalment, the same instalment is available again for borrowing
- Cash loans work much the same way except they are more expensive
- If you have allowed yourself to depend on the recycling debt, it is harder to get out of it
- As long as these loans are used for survival, they will remain addictive

16. What Is the Best Way to Get Out of the Cash Loan Cycle?

- The best way to get out debt is to pay and never go back
- Set up an automatic debt repayment plan and stick to it
- Cut up credit cards and never buy on line using a credit card, rather use debit cards because you can
- Don't top up any loans

- To speed up your payments, create new money and direct it towards your loans
- When you are done with loans, focus on sending money to yourself through investments
- Remember yourself
- Include yourself among those you love.
- Build your assets and your investments. That is what matters more than spending time dealing with other people's money.

Acknowledgements

The recreation of this book series was as a result of the revision of *Functional Mastery Over My Finances*. We created a course that got accredited by Botswana Qualifications Authority (BQA). We needed a more relevant "text book" that could accompany the course.

Once I had ploughed through the material, my colleague and fellow personal finance educator Poloko Mongatane was a great help in not only pushing for the accreditation of the course, but getting her hands dirty and helping to create some of the assessment questions at the end of some of the chapters, as well as doing some editing.

The book series idea came in a bit to reduce the book to chewable chunks instead of one big bite. While all the three books in the series are contained in this one volume, a person could choose to read any of the books in any order.

Great thanks to all the people who have given feedback since the publication of the first book in 2008. Many thanks also to all the workshop participants who brought in new perspectives on some of the concepts and for helping to improve them.

Many thanks to my staff at Moedi Financial Training for their constant support. Oteng "Owty" Orakanye, many of the workshops that have happened to improve this material would not have happened without you.

My gratitude goes to my family always for their unending support.

Thank you

Nelson Letshwene

About the Author

Nelson Letshwene is the author of several books including *Faith and Purpose – Living Life to the full without Fear, Guilt, or Regrets*. He is also the author of *Your Longing Is Your Calling – Finding your Purpose through the seven desires of life*.

He holds a bachelors degree in business economics from The University of the Witwatersrand (Wits) (Johannesburg), and an Honours degree from The University of South Africa (UNISA).

Nelson is the founder and managing director of Moedi Learning Technologies, which focuses on financial education.

He is a speaker on Financial and Functional literacy issues. He writes for several newspapers and magazines on personal finance issues. He hosts several radio shows focusing on personal finance.

For more please visit his website on

www.nelsonletshwene.com

Or his Money Skills blog on
www.7moneyskills.wordpress.com
www.thegoldenruleblog.wordpess.com
Like his Facebook page:
Money Skills with Nelson Letshwene

Follow him on twitter @101silverline or @NLetshwene

BIBLIOGRAPHY

1. Abraham Jay, 1995, 2002, 9 Pillars to business growth, Torrance, CA,Abraham Publishing group, Inc.
2. Berger Rob, Top 100 Money Quotes of all time, www.forbes.com
3. Cameron, B. 2003. Getting Started: Money Matters for Under 25s. Cape Town: Zebra Press
4. Cameron, B. 2003. Massive fraud in funeral assurance industry exposed. Personal Finance: 1, August 9.
5. Cameron, B. 2003. Steep rise in lapsed policies. Personal Finance:1. September 27.
6. Clark, J.B. 1990. Marketing Today – Successes, Failures, and Turnarounds, 2nd eds. New Jersey: Prentice-Hall Inc.
7. Clason George S, 1926, The Richest Man in Babylon, Penguin books
8. Griffin, G. Edward, 1994, The Creature from Jekyll Island, American Media
9. Hartmann Thom, The Last Hours of Ancient Sunlight, Three Rivers Press, NY, 2004
10. Hill, Napolean, 1937, Think and Grow Rich, Fawcett books, New York
11. Johnson, S. Et al. 1999. Saving Faith. Boston: DPI
12. Kiyosaki, R.T and Lechter, S.L 1997. Rich Dad

Poor Dad, - what the rich teach their kids about money that the poor and middle class do not. New York, Warner Books Inc.

13. Kiyosaki, R.T and Lechter, S.L 1999. Cashflow Quadrant, New York, Warner Books Inc
14. Kiyosaki, R.T and Lechter, S.L 2000. Rich Dad's Guide to becoming rich, without cutting up your credit cards. New York. Warner Audio Books.
15. Kiyosaki, R.T and Lechter, S.L 2000. Rich Dad's Guide to Investing. New York. Warner Books.
16. Kiyosaki, R.T and Lechter, S.L 2001-2005, The Business School, 2nd ed, Momentum Media.
17. Kiyosaki, R.T and Lechter, S.L 2008, Increase Your Financial IQ, New York, Business Plus
18. Landsburg, Steven, E, 1993, The Armchair Economist, Simon & Schuster, London
19. Langemeier, Loral, 2005, The Millionaire Maker, McGraw-Hill
20. Langemeier, Loral, 2007, The Millionaire Maker's Guide to creating a Cash Machine for life, McGraw-Hill
21. Langemeier, Loral, 2009, Put More Cash in your Pocket: Turn what you know into dough, Harper Paperbacks
22. Lechter, M, Other People's Money, Warner Books, New York
23. Letshwene, R.N, 2008, Functional Mastery Over My Finances, Reach Publishers
24. Letshwene, R.N. 2004, UNISA, Personal Financial Management in Botswana
25. Letshwene, R.N. 2010, The Retirement Report, Moedi Publishing, Gaborone

26. Letshwene, R.N. 2011, Mastery Over Debt (Audio) Moedi Publishing, Gaborone
27. Letshwene, R.N. 2013, The Savings Report, Moedi Publishing, Gaborone
28. Masterson, M. 2005. Automatic Wealth – the 6 steps to financial independence. New Jersey: John Wiley & Sons Inc.
29. Orman, S. 2001. The Road to Wealth- a comprehensive guide to your money.
30. Orman, S. 2003. The Laws of Money, the lessons of life. New York. Simon & Schuster Inc. (Audio book)
31. Patel, Raj, 2009, The Value of Nothing, Portobello books.
32. Perkins, J. 2004, Confessions of an Economic Hitman, Penguin
33. Stanley Thomas, J, and Danko William, D, 1996, The Millionaire Next Door, Pocket Books, New York
34. Swart, N.J. 2003, Personal Financial Management, the Southern African guide to personal financial planning, 2nd Edition, Lansdowne: Juta
35. Swart, N.J. 2003, Starting and buying your own business in a franchise, Cape Town: Juta
36. Templar, R. 2012, The Rules of Wealth, Pearson, London.
37. Wilde Stuart, 1989, The Trick to Money is having some! Hay House, London
38. www.7moneyskills.wordpress.com
39. www.Investopedia.com
40. www.nelsonletshwene.com

Nelson Letshwene

RECOMMENDED READING

1. Born Rich by Bob Proctor
2. Conversations with God , by Neale Donald Walsch
3. Seven Essential Money Skills, by Nelson Letshwene
4. Rich Dad Poor Dad, by Robert Kiyosaki
5. The Millionaire Maker, Loral Langemeier
6. The One-minute millionaire, by Robert Allen & Mark Victor Hansen
7. The Richest Man in Babylon, by George Clason
8. The Science of Getting Rich, by Wallace D. Wattles
9. The Strangest Secret, by Earl Nightingale (audio program)
10. Think and Grow Rich, by Napoleon Hill
11. The Millionaire Next Door, by Thomas J Stanley and William D Danko

Other Books By NELSON LETSHWENE

Book Title	Description
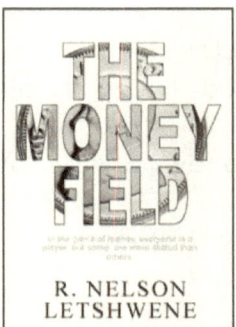	***The Money Field*** is like a sports field upon which the game of money is played. In its four quadrants are various players including yourself. Each player's goal is to win. This book gives you the rules, winning strategies and how others play against you. Will you win this game? The money game is life's compulsory game. Time to play and win!
	These Money skills are to be installed, activated, and practiced transforming you and your relationship with your money. Learn skills to create multiple streams of income, to save and invest, to protect and build controls, to build long lasting value and to share your bounty with others. Everyone who handles money must have these skills

The Money Field book series – 3-in-1

Book Title	Description
MY MONEY MY POWER — R Nelson Letshwene	Your money came to you in exchange for your power: be that skill, talent, idea, or sweat. It remains your responsibility to keep that power. It is easy to lose your power to the commercial system and be a slave to lenders and traders. You only retain your power when you turn your money into investments and assets that produce more income. This book is about leading your money through decisive actions to retain your power.
If We Were All #Financially_Literate — 49 VIRTUES OF FINANCIAL KNOWLEDGE — R NELSON LETSHWENE	This book is a thought stimulator – to get us to think about areas of our financial literacy. You may be good in one but lack in another. Earnings; controls; our psychology of money; debt; savings; investments; assets; etc. Take the journey.

Book Title	Description
FAITH and PURPOSE LIVING LIFE TO THE FULL WITHOUT FEAR, GUILT, OR REGRETS R NELSON LETSHWENE	The question of what faith is, has kept truth seekers on the path for centuries. Faith is both Art and Science. It is the process of becoming one with your desires and with the creator. Faith is a force in the universe that can make things happen. Purpose if faith with passion. Take this journey now.
Your Longing Is Your Calling How to find your Purpose through the Seven Desires of Life R Nelson Letshwene	What is a calling? A Longing; a pining; a wish; a yearning; a hunger; a lust; a craving; an aching, a desire! Life is calling you to live it to the full. The Call will keep ringing until it is answered. Desire is a propensity to grow. Follow the Seven rivers of desire flowing within your being.

All these available on www.amazon.com

THANK YOU

If you enjoyed reading this book, please feel free to leave me a review. Reviews help other readers to know the relevance of the book for them and they help authors like me to improve on our work for the benefit of our readers.

Nelson Letshwene

Nelson@moedi.net
Twit: @NLetshwene and/or @101Silverline
#TheMoneyField